In the SHELTER of EACH OTHER

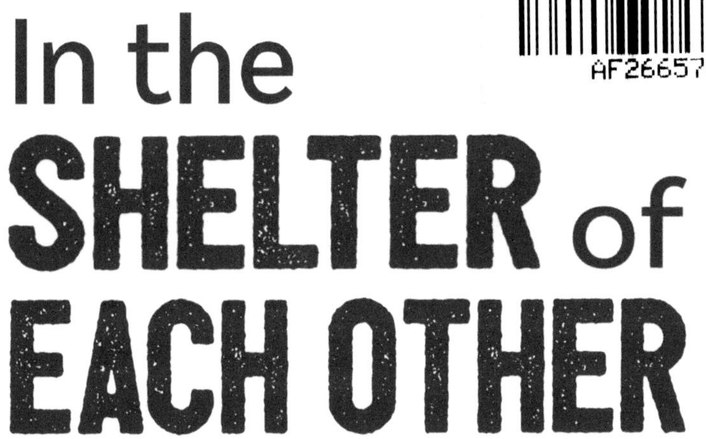

Photos & Stories

CATHRYN WELLNER

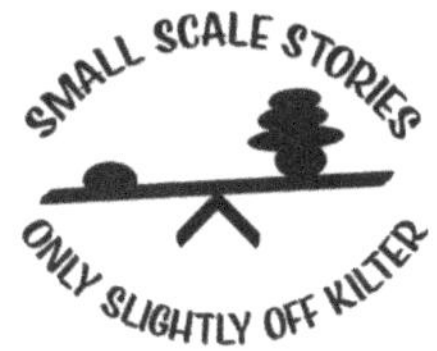

Small Scale Stories #4

Espoir Press

British Columbia 2017

Espoir Press
1002 - 1128 Sunset Drive
Kelowna, British Columbia
Canada V1Y 9W7

In the Shelter of Each Other (Small Scale Stories #4)

ISBN 978-1-988760-05-6

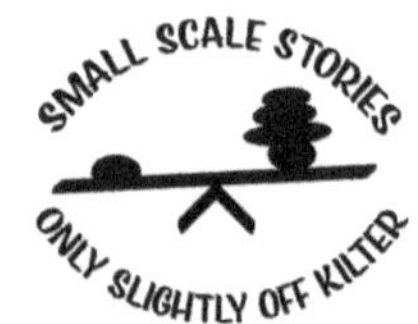

INTRODUCTION

If you daydream, you will find friends in this book. If you talk to ducks and are sure you are communicating, you belong to the tribe. If clouds tell you stories, your mind is getting exercise it needs to stay sharp. If you believe everything is alive and is counting on you, you are connected to the universe in ways that are good for the planet.

You have imagination. You are creative. You don't think outside the box. You were never inside it. You see the world edgewise and are entirely comfortable with that. Small Scale Stories are for you.

In this fourth collection of Small Scale Stories, you will meet a contented beaver, a feather determined to help find a lost puppy, a rope and a stick becoming fast friends, a leaf trying to organize a symphony, a philosopher dog and many other offbeat characters. They will seem entirely familiar to you because you have met many just like them.

You see dogs, trees, stones, ducks and people as interconnected. You understand we have more genes in common with each other than we have differences. So pick up this book, kick back and relax. You are among friends, and we are only slightly off kilter.

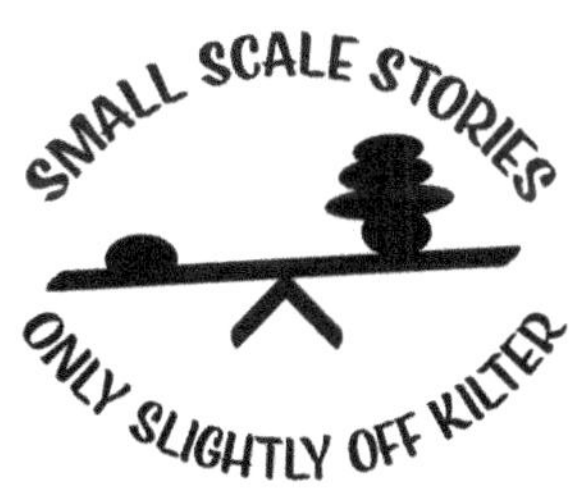

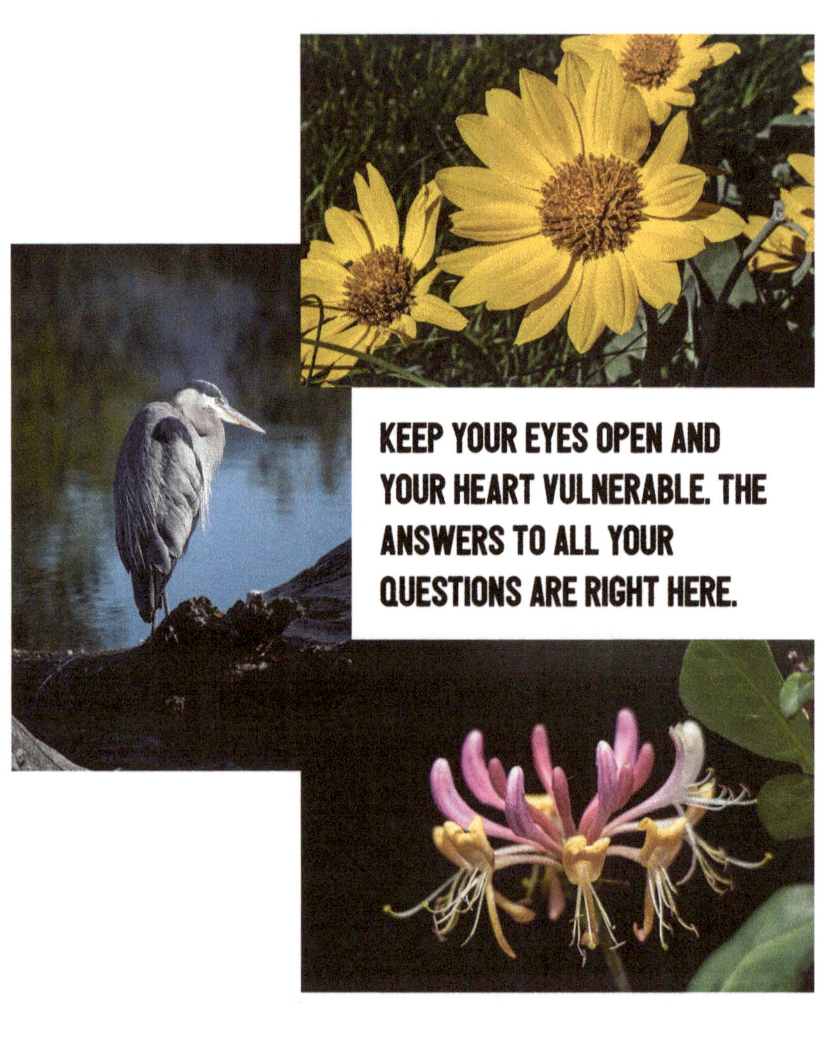
KEEP YOUR EYES OPEN AND YOUR HEART VULNERABLE. THE ANSWERS TO ALL YOUR QUESTIONS ARE RIGHT HERE.

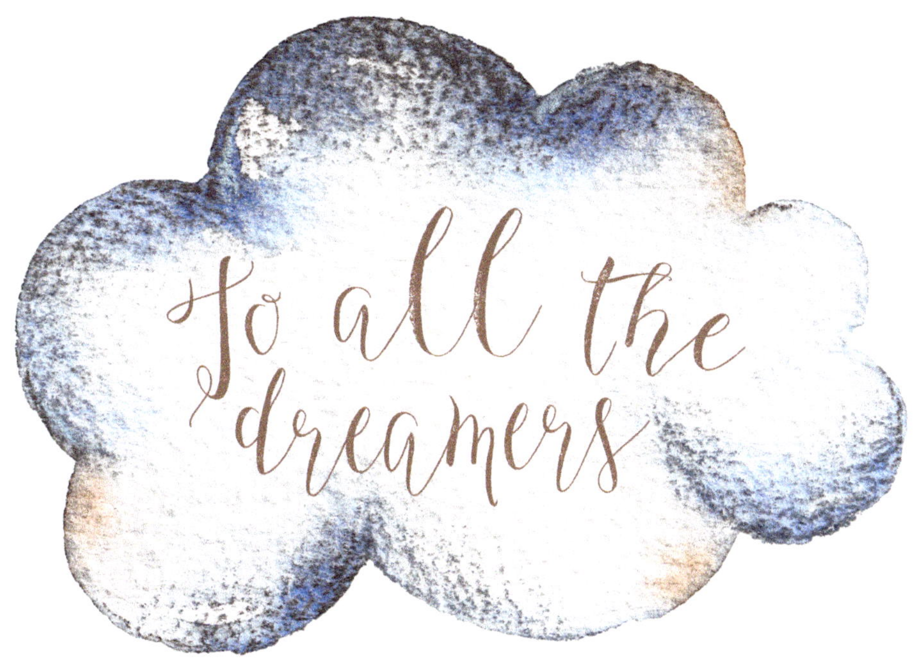

With your feet on the ground and
your head in the clouds, you see so
much more of what is really going
on in this beautiful world we share.

THE STORIES

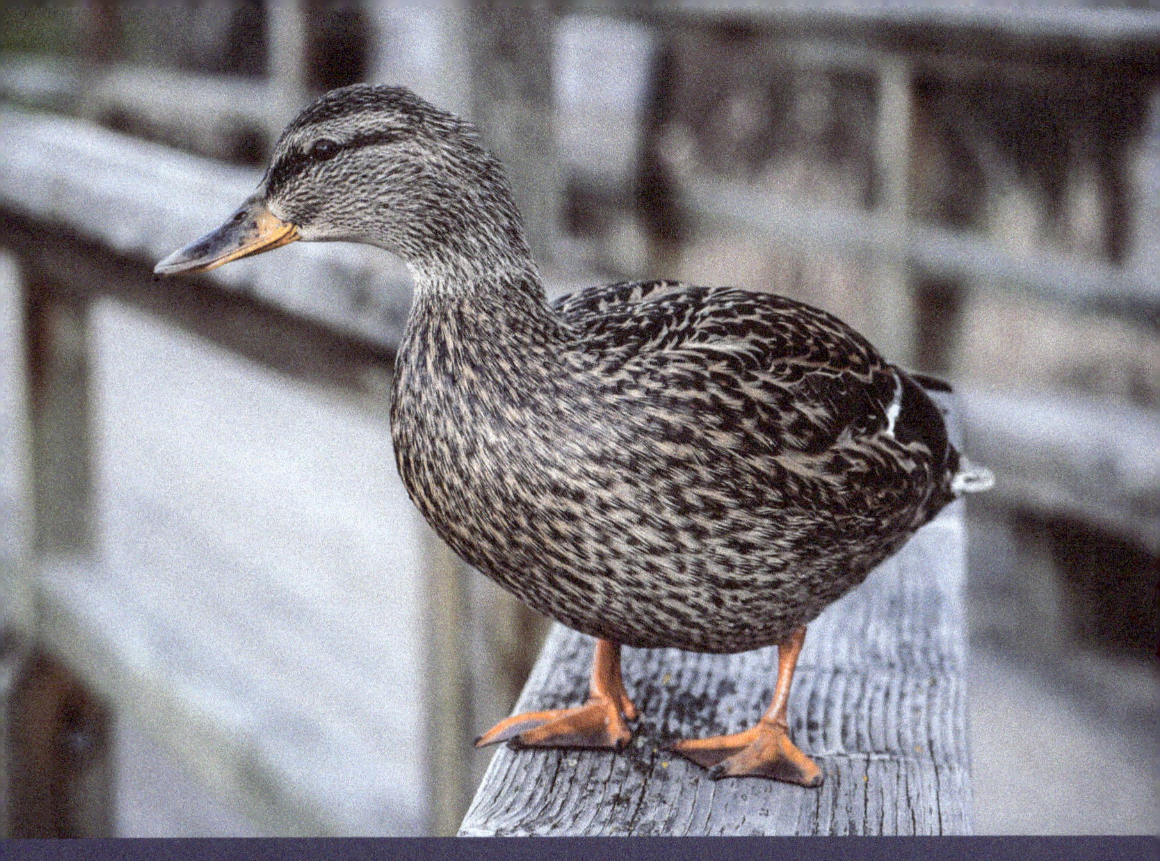

"How very curious," thought Duck. "Seed Bringer changes her skin a lot. I'm sure yesterday she had on a red skin. Today it's green. Humans are so unpredictable."

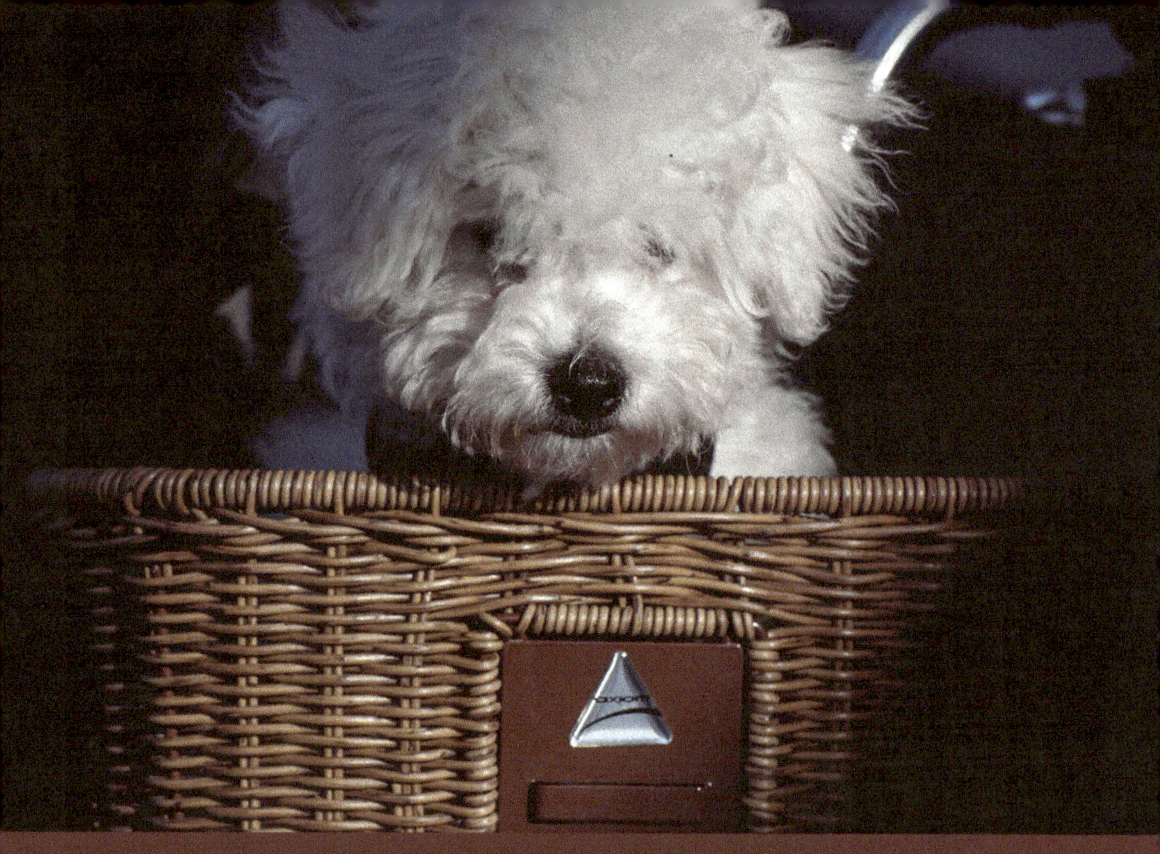

Dog was philosophical about this basket business. He preferred to run, but his human rode her bicycle so fast he could not keep up.

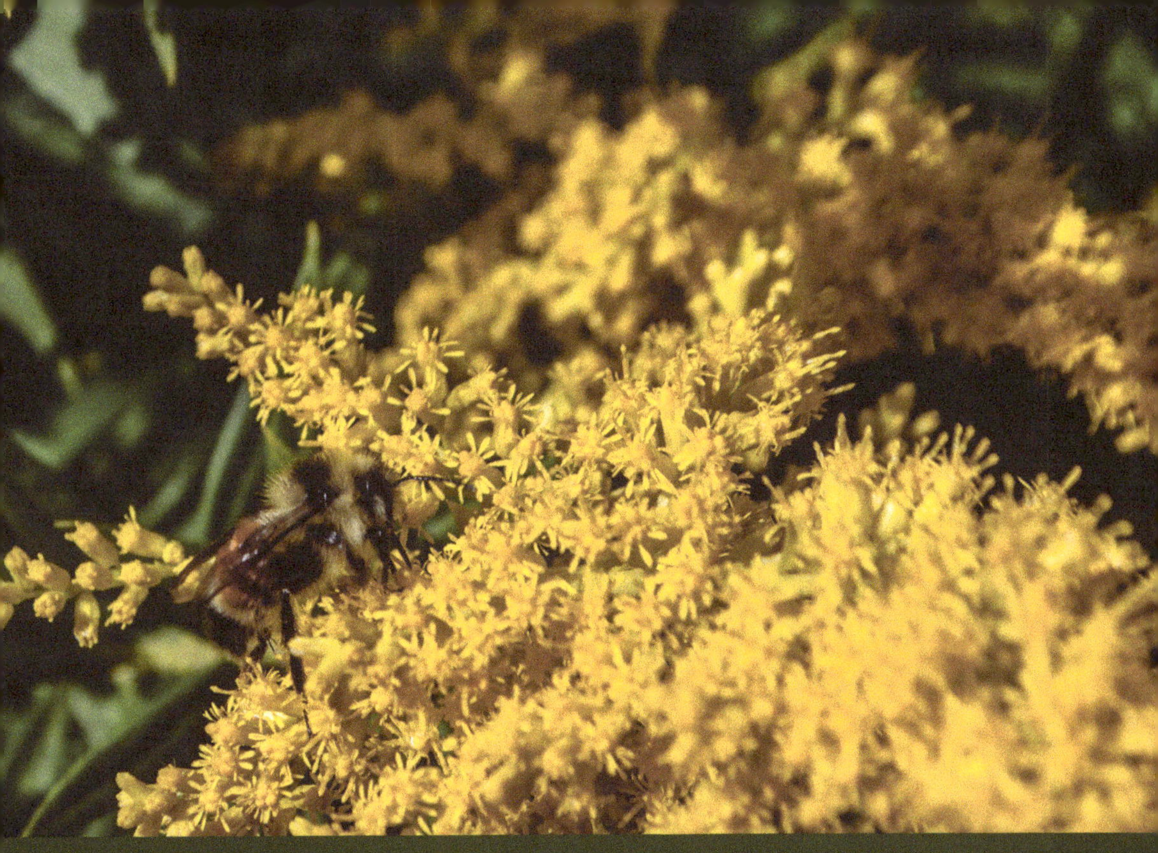

"Pick me, pick me," cried hundreds of tiny goldenrod blossoms. Bee tried to visit every flower, but his legs grew heavy with pollen, and he flew back to the hive.

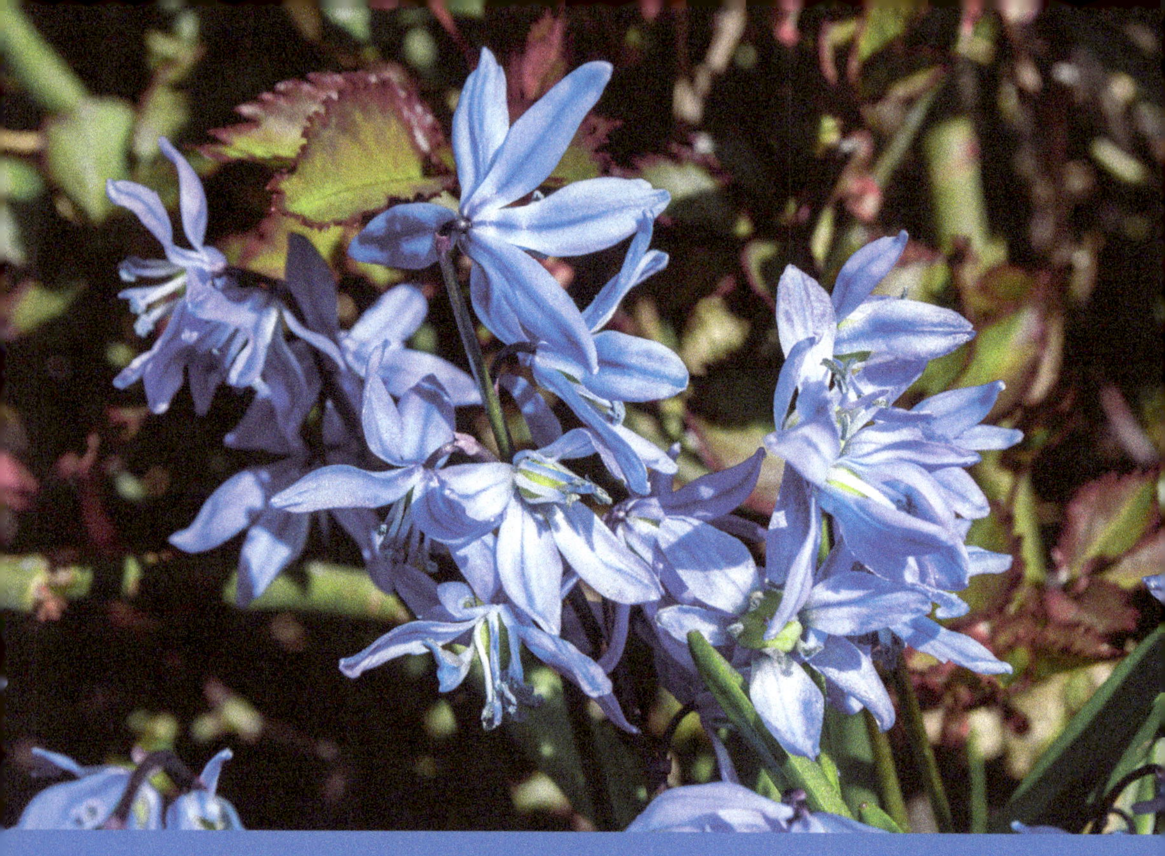

The Scilla sisters slept quietly through the winter. When they felt the soil around them warm, they burst into bloom.

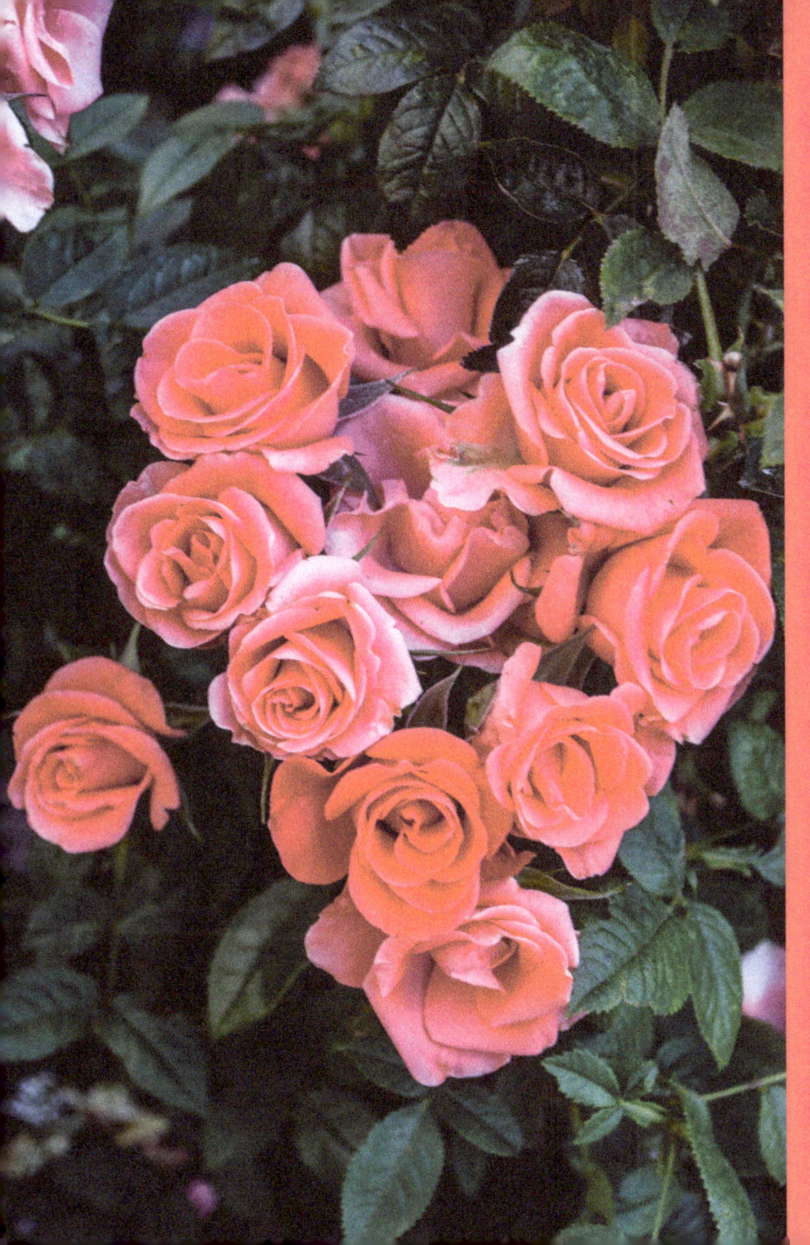

The Rose Bunch decided to try something new this year. They would grow tightly together and offer a perfect bouquet. They hadn't counted on Mazie's blooming early or Shirleen's petal going brown.

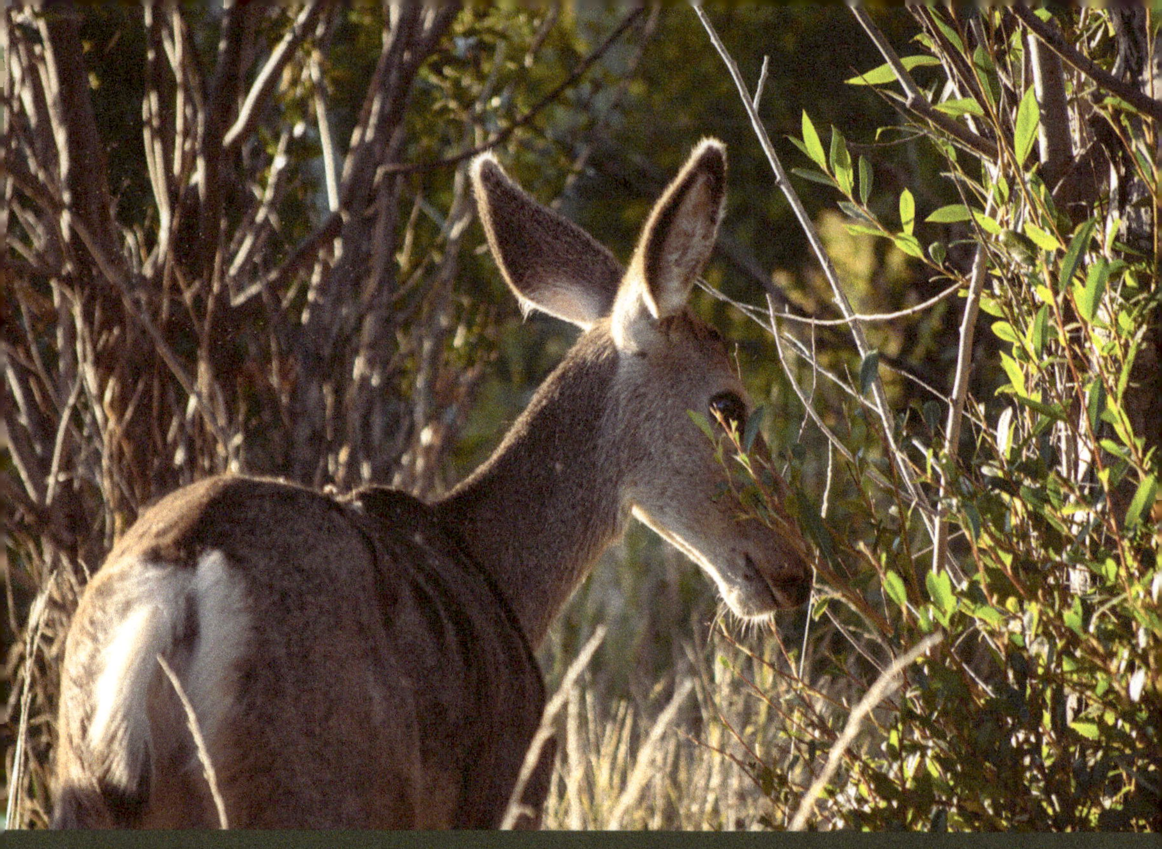

"Thanks for hanging around, Willow," said Deer.
"OK for you," grumbled Willow. "You're not being
eaten." Then Willow remembered her leaves
would soon fall anyway. "You're welcome, Deer,"
she said.

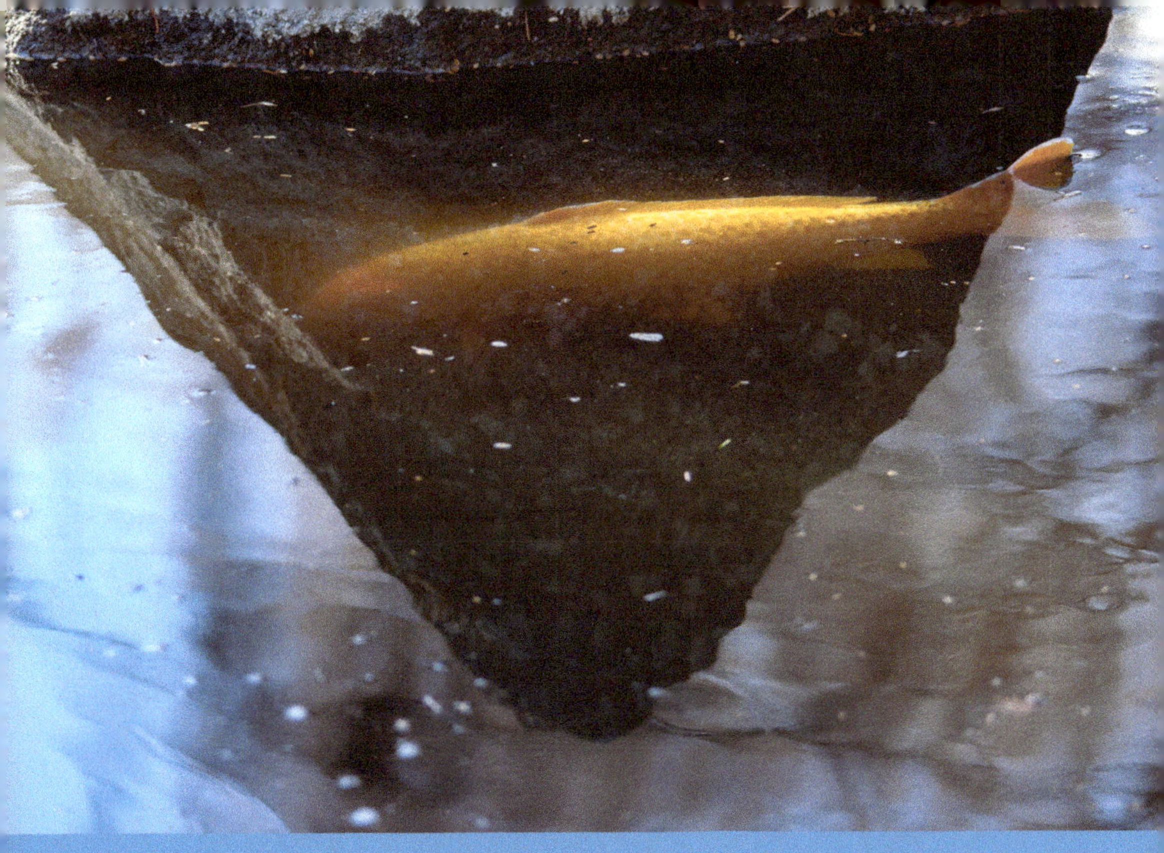

The golden fish had heard of the magic of
pyramids and wondered if it would work for her.

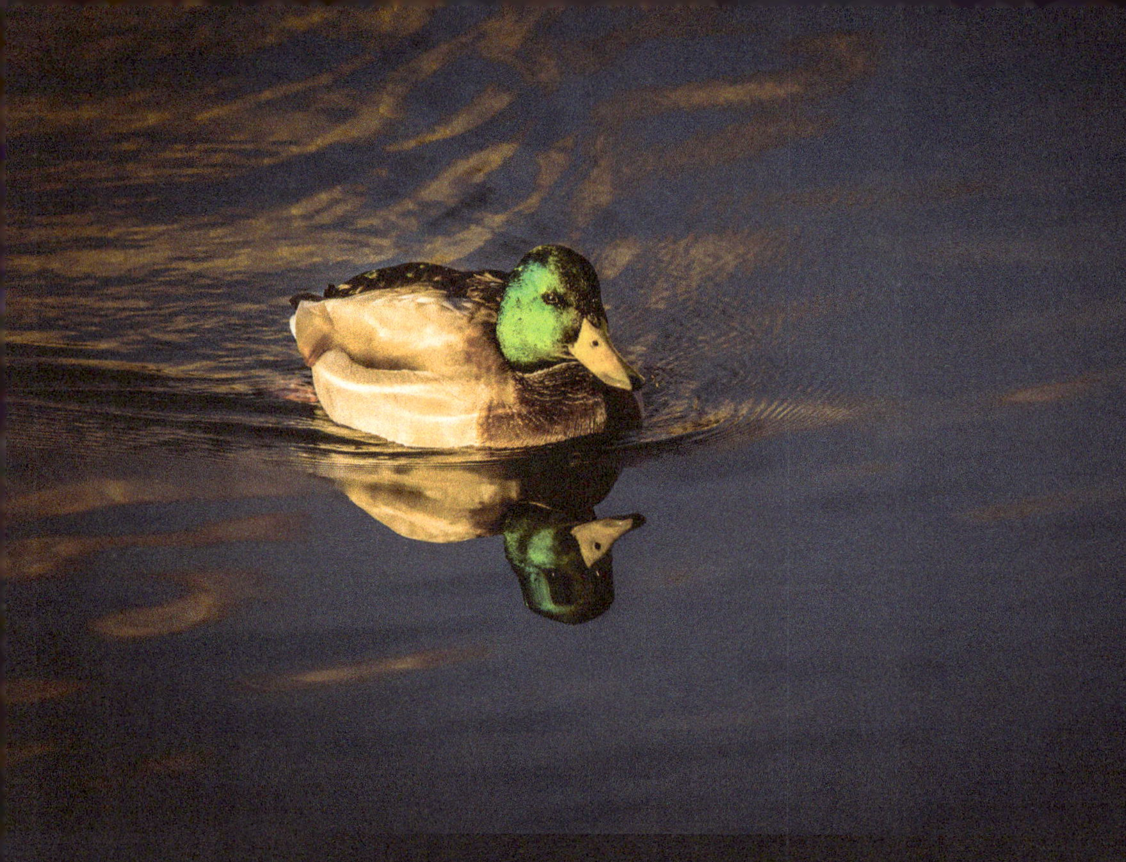

Mallard wondered why humans kept bringing odd things to their eyes and pointing at him. He knew nothing about smart phones and cameras, nor about the play of sun on his feathers. He did know humans had strange habits.

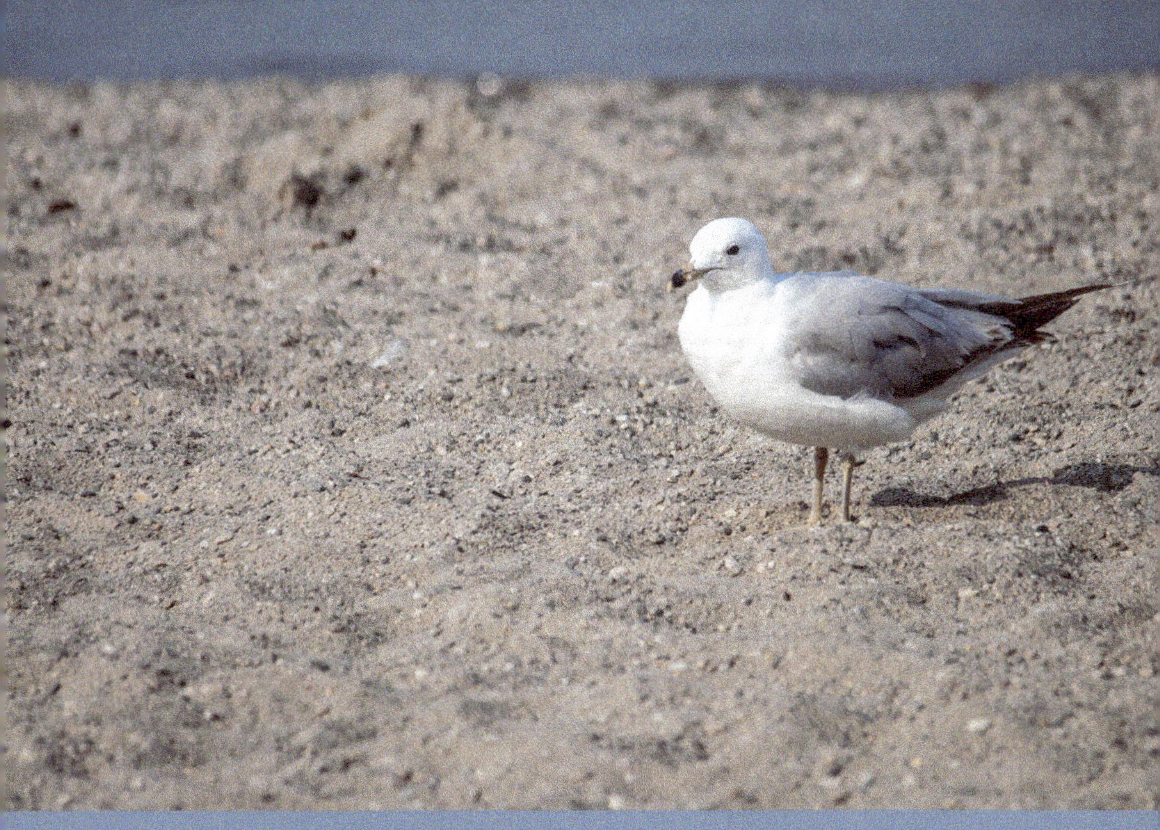

"Singing in the sand, just singing in the sand. What a glorious feeling..." Gull sang the bird version, though his mates laughed at him. He did not care. He sang for joy, not for praise.

Butterfly
agreed to
judge the
rhodie
costumes
this year.
No one
thought to
ask if he
could tell
one
blossom
from
another.

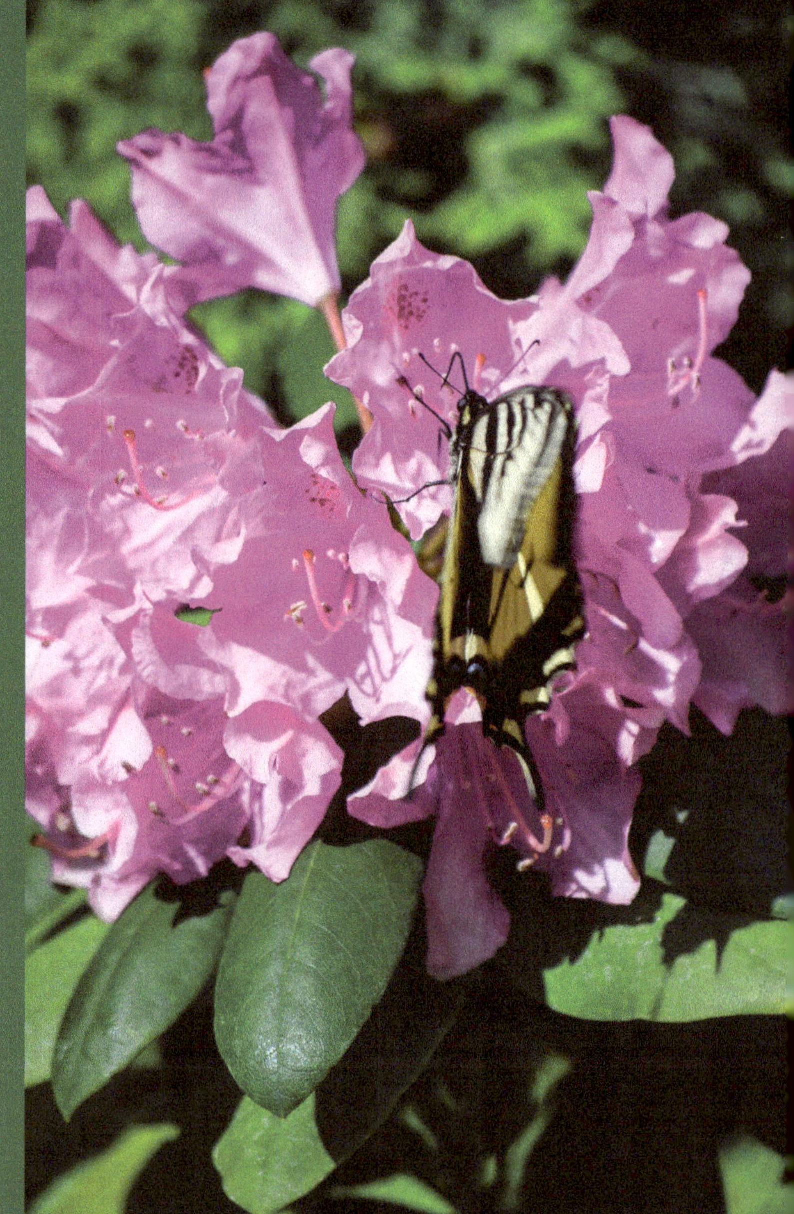

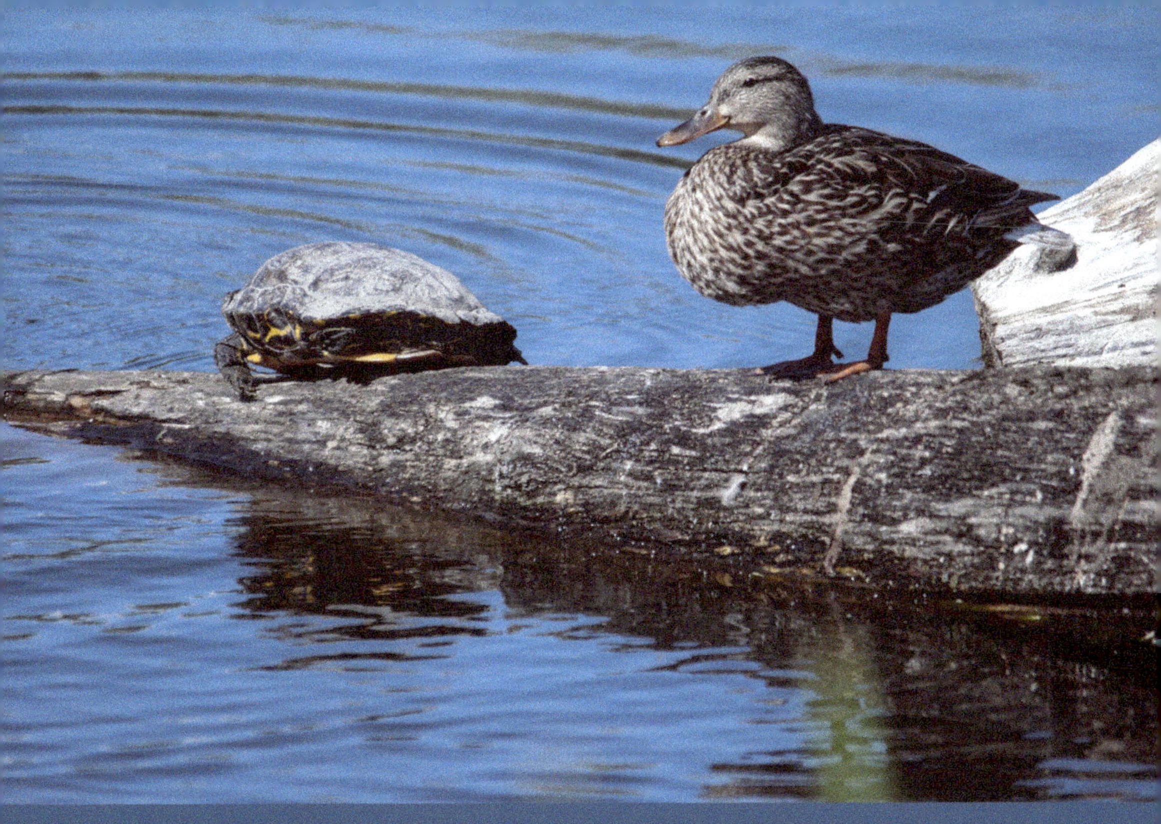

Duck could never listen quietly to wind and water. She loved the sound of her quacks. Turtle liked her company but longed for silence so slipped off the log and swam away.

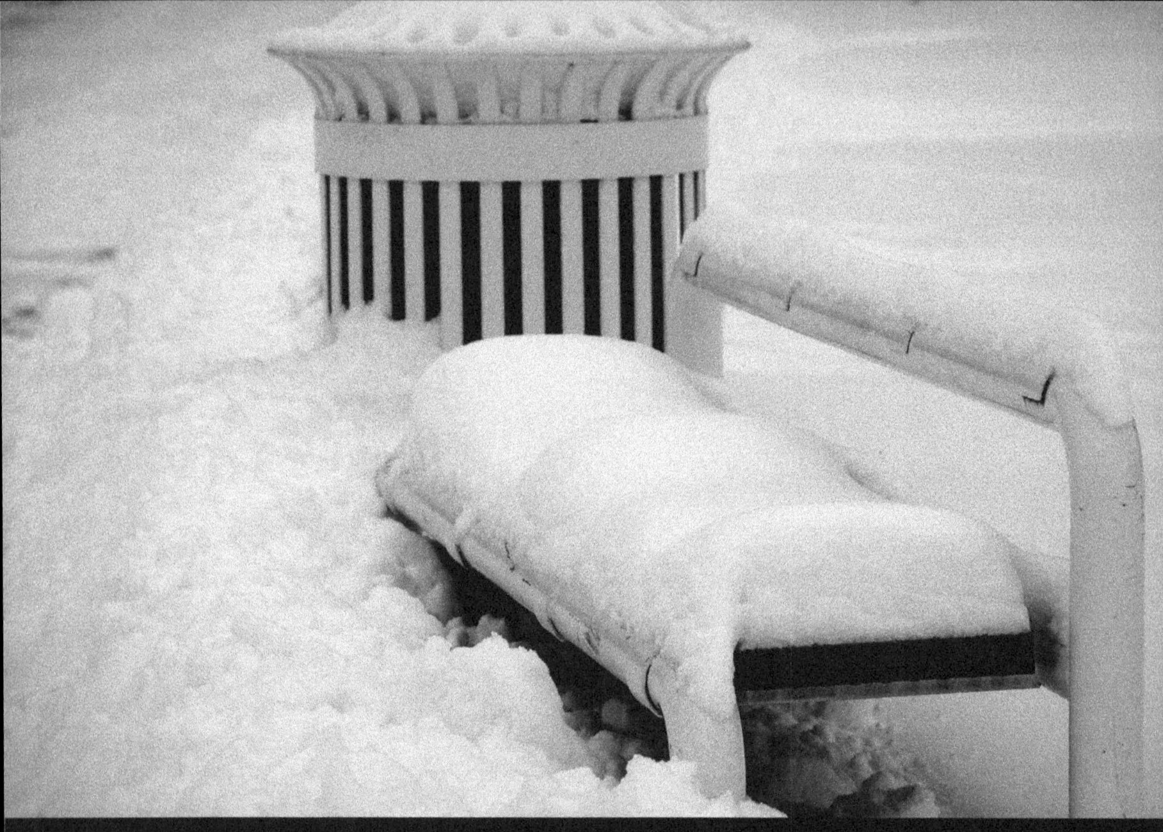

Garbage Can could see Bench was getting sentimental about the warm bums of summer. "Cheer up, Pal. Remember the farters."

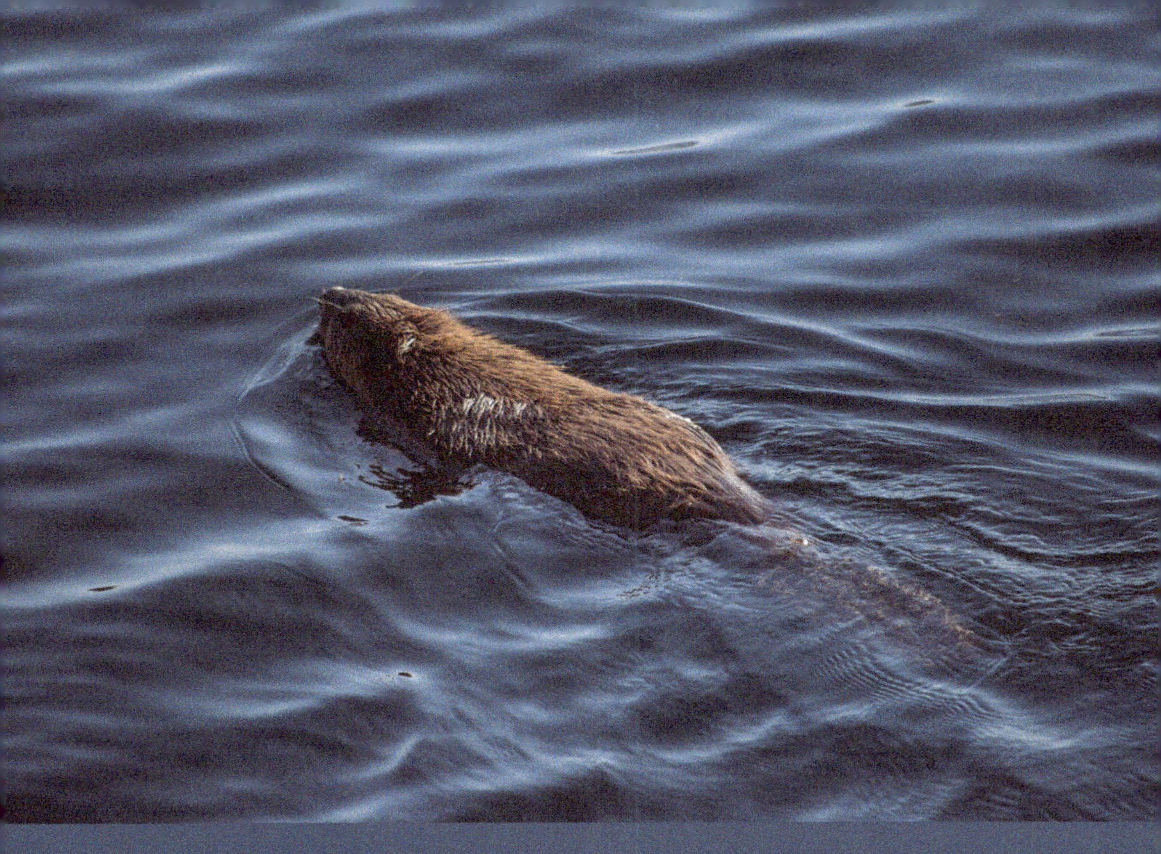

Beaver knew every inch of the lake bottom, where succulent plants were plentiful. He knew the best rocks to sit on while he ate them. Life was good.

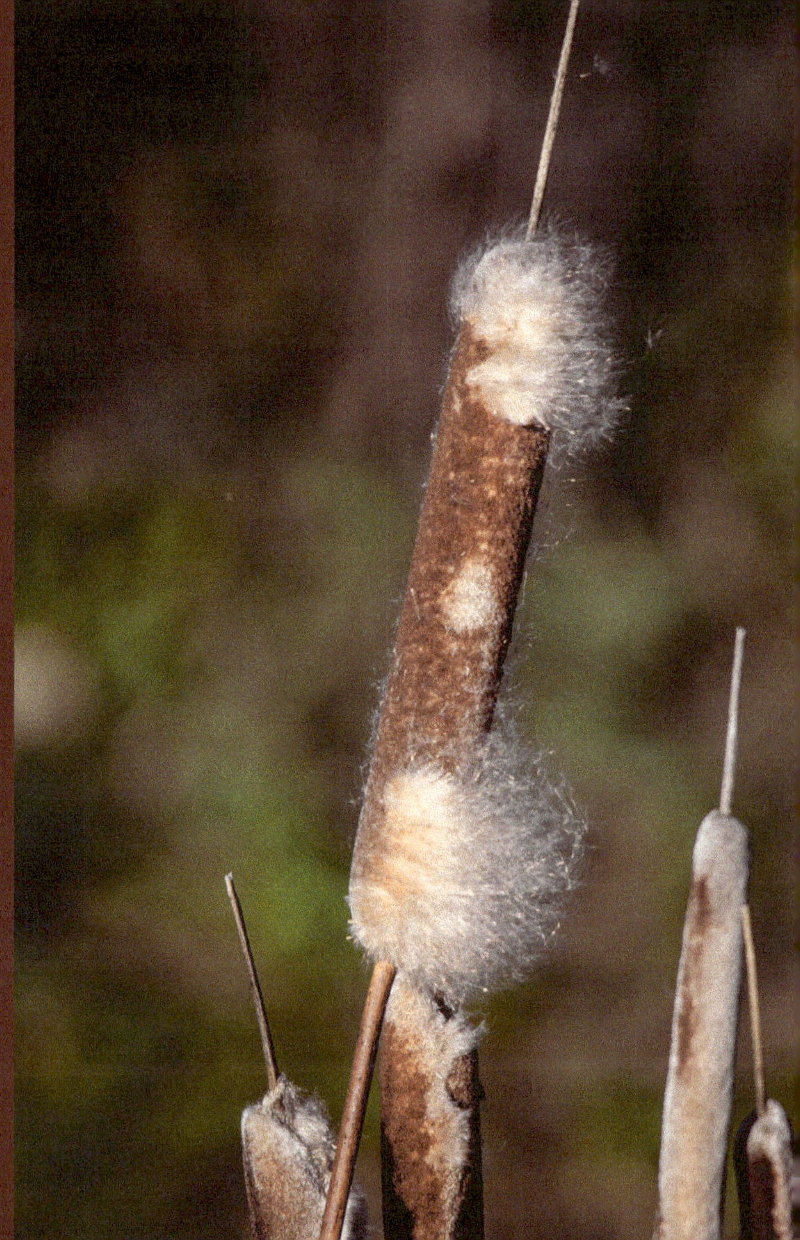

"Wind loved playing with the cattails, expecially in autumn, when they dried out. He was quite the artist. He was aiming for an Elvis Presley look with this one and laughed when he saw the big bum.

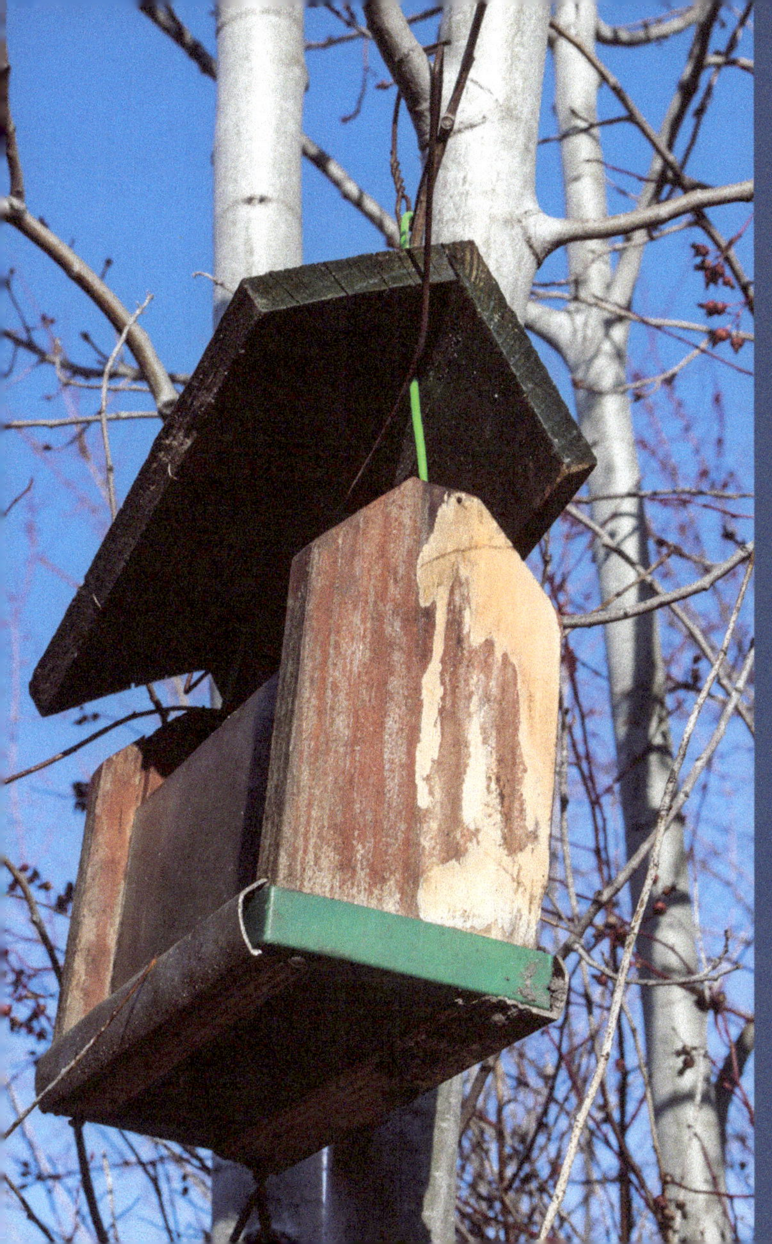

Bird Feeder kept trying to get the humans to help him out. His roof was askew. He wanted it fixed before some young bird got trapped inside his belly.

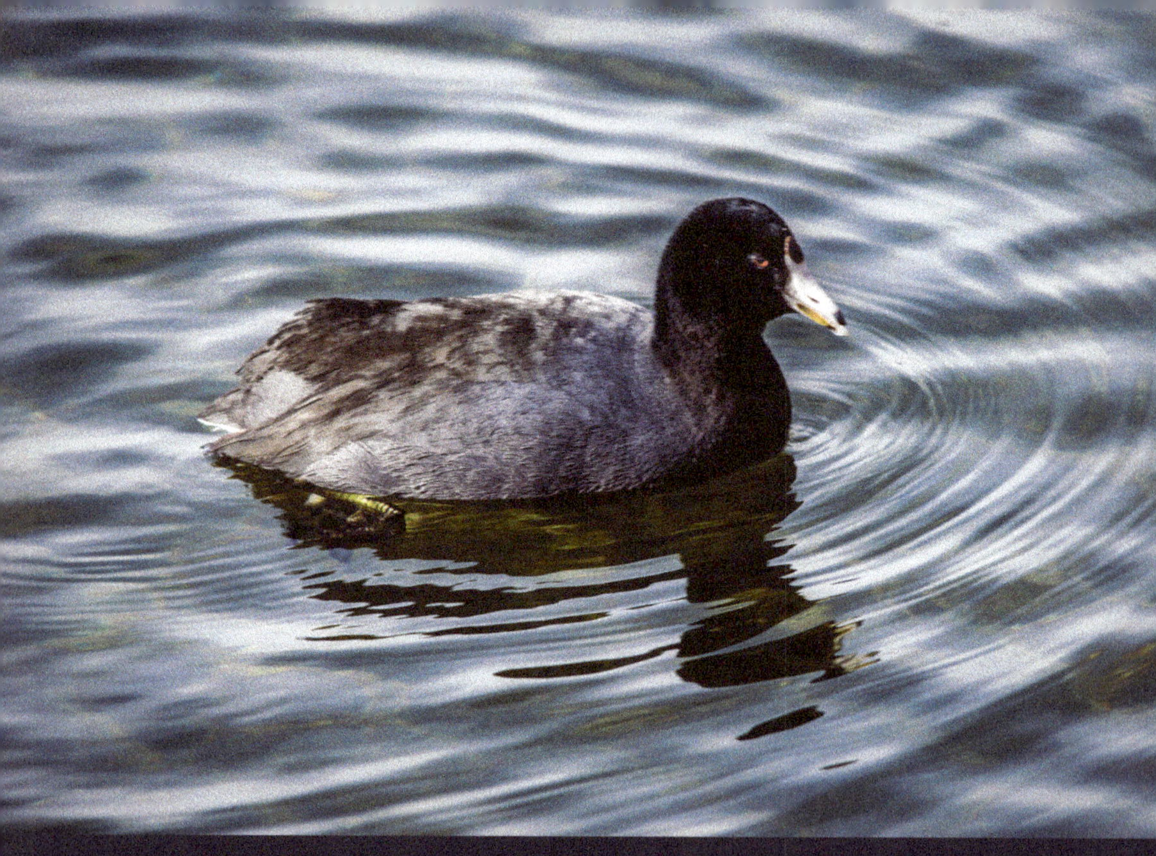

Coot might have contemplated the meaning of life had he not been certain it was about food, safety and sex. That left him free to simply sit and stare.

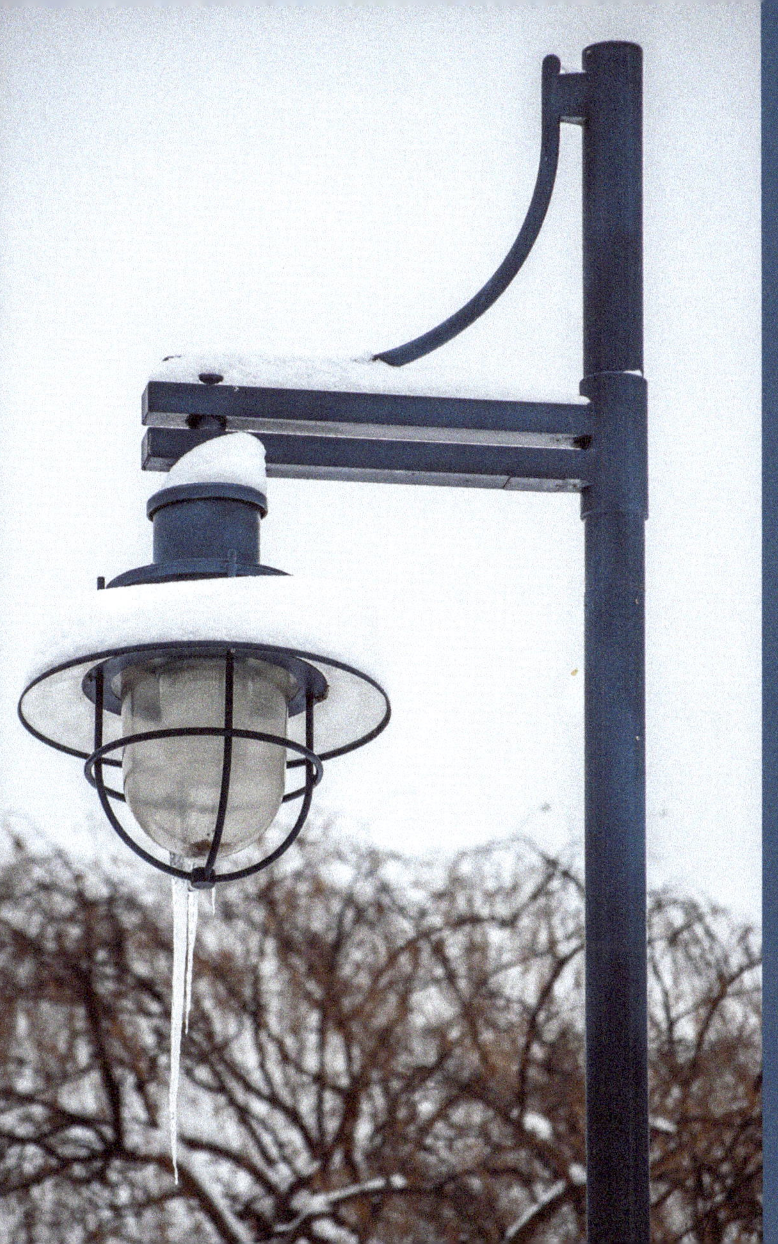

Lamp was pleased with her ice whiskers. She used them to try out different roles. This morning she was a wise old man, advising passing couples on their love lives.

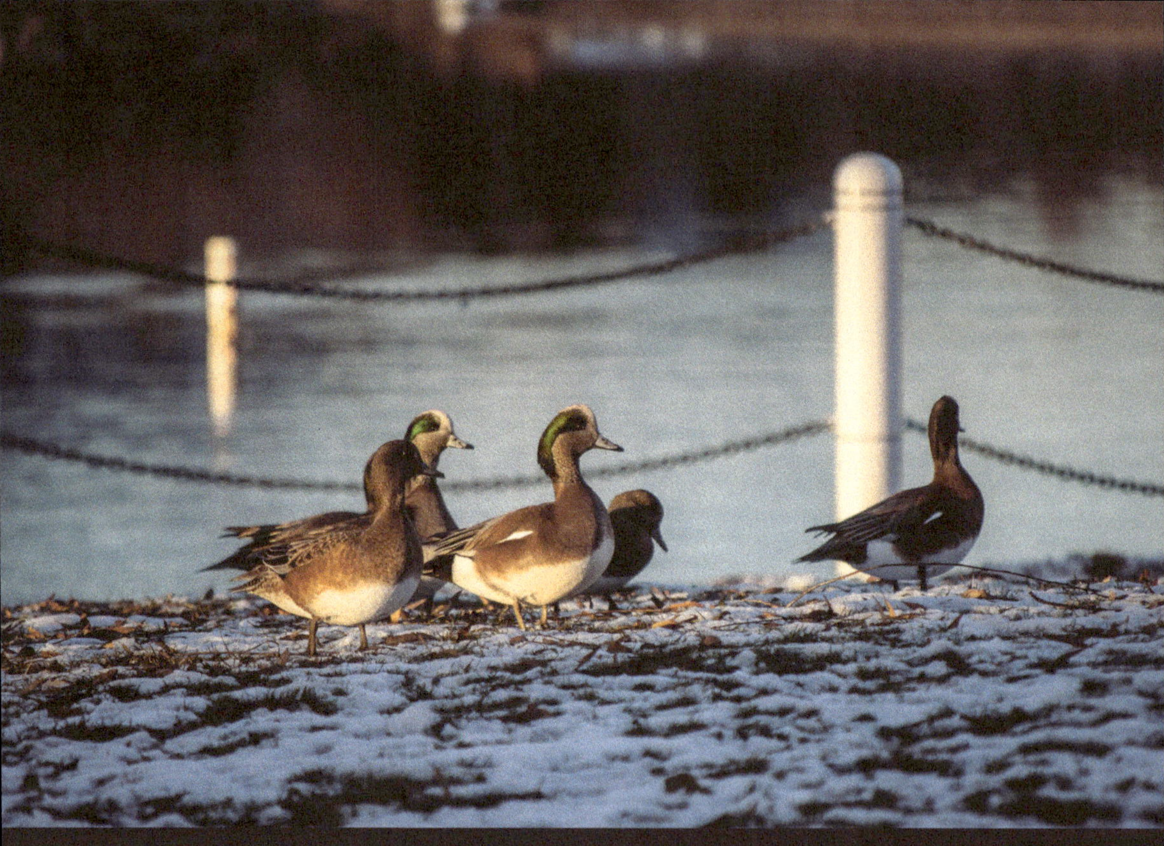

After a day of grazing, the wigeons turned toward home. They knew "home" had shifting meaning, depending on season, time of day, and safety. Tonight they would sleep in the shelter of each other.

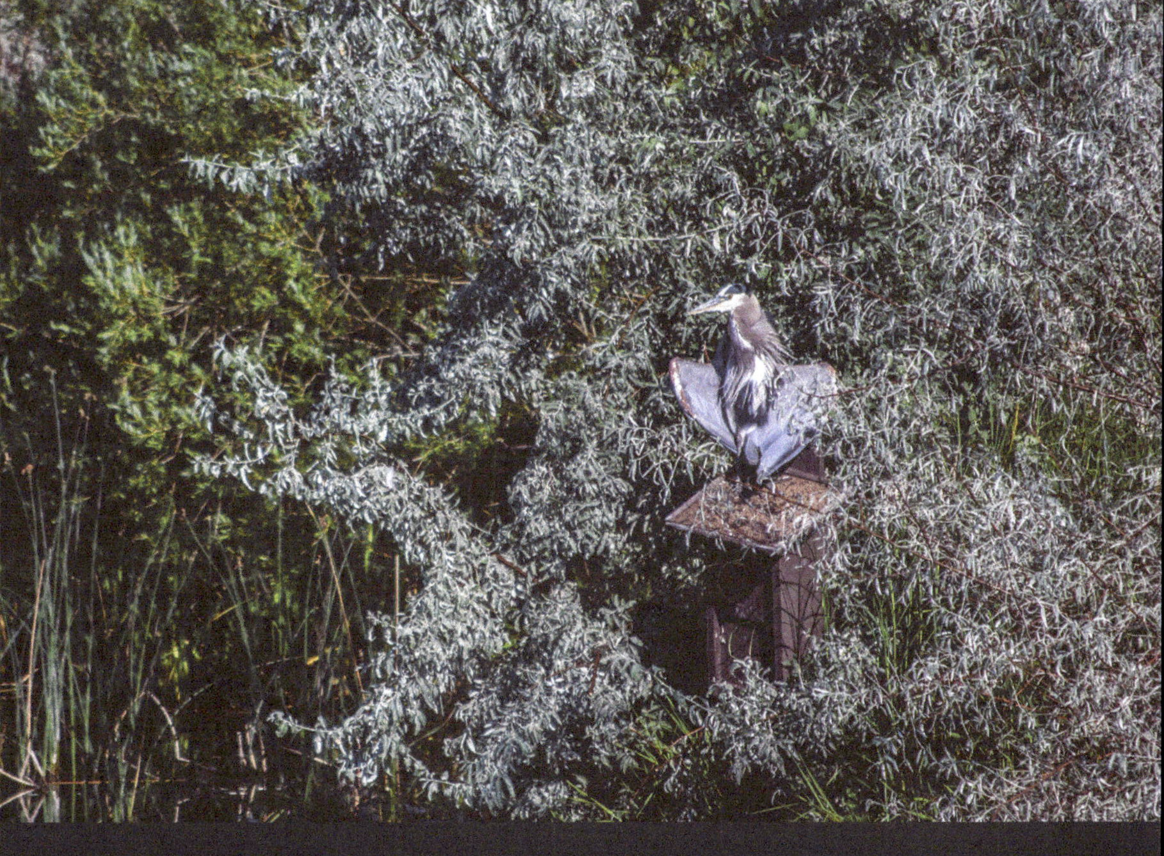

Camouflaged by the Russian olives, Heron unleashed his Wild Dancer spirit.

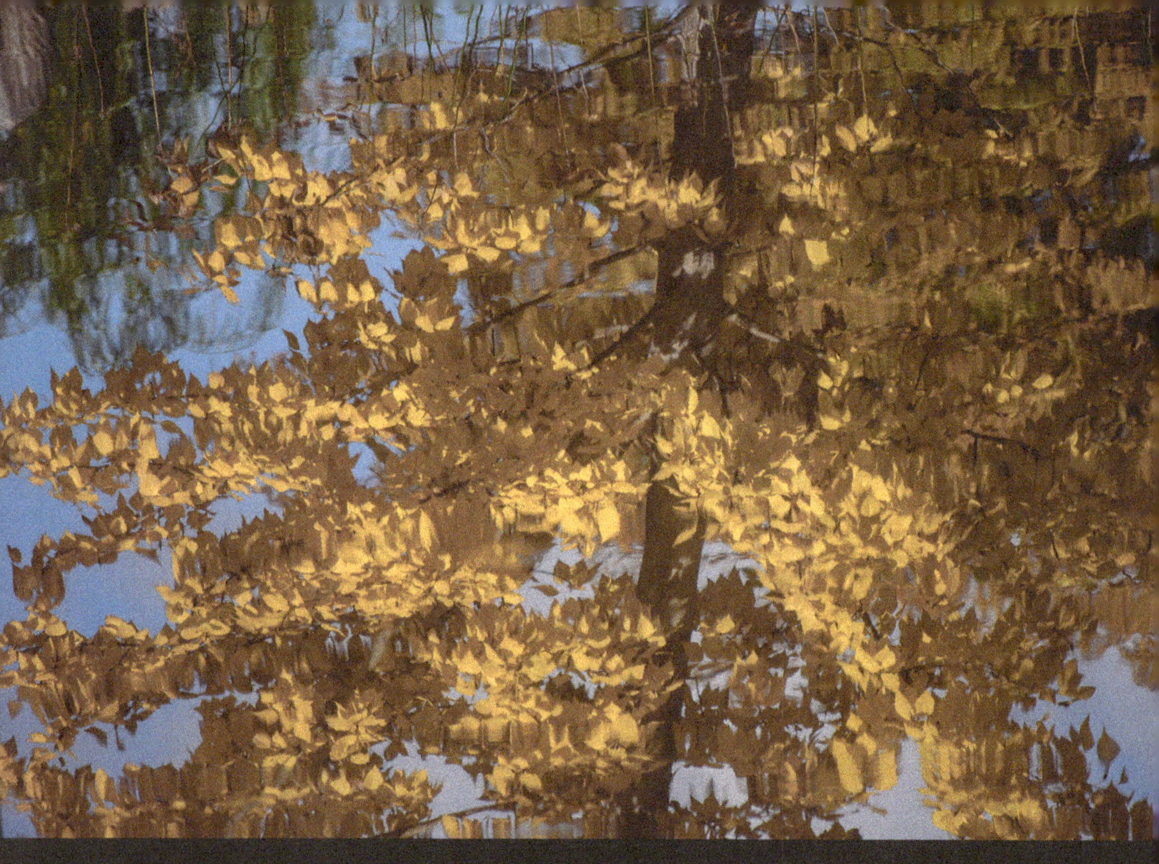

If it hadn't been for the telltale ripples around her lower leaves, Tree might have been so startled by her perfect reflection she would have toppled into the water.

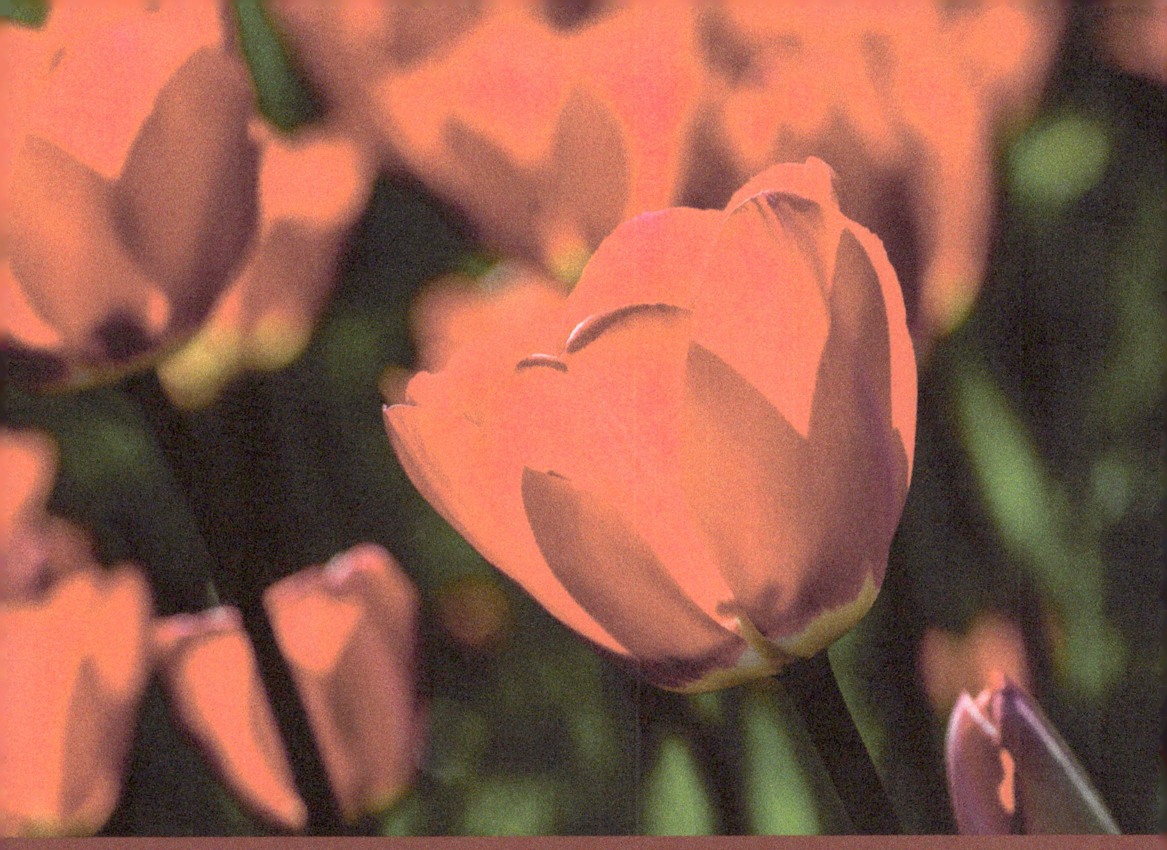

She leaned her face toward the sun, loving the bright rays. To be part of the annual celebration of life and renewal was her greatest joy.

He had felt
useful, filled
with apples and
chips. But as
soon as they
emptied him at
the picnic, they
tossed him
away. Wind
blew him into a
tree, where he
caught on a
branch. He tried
to be friendly,
but no one
seemed
interested in
getting to know
him.

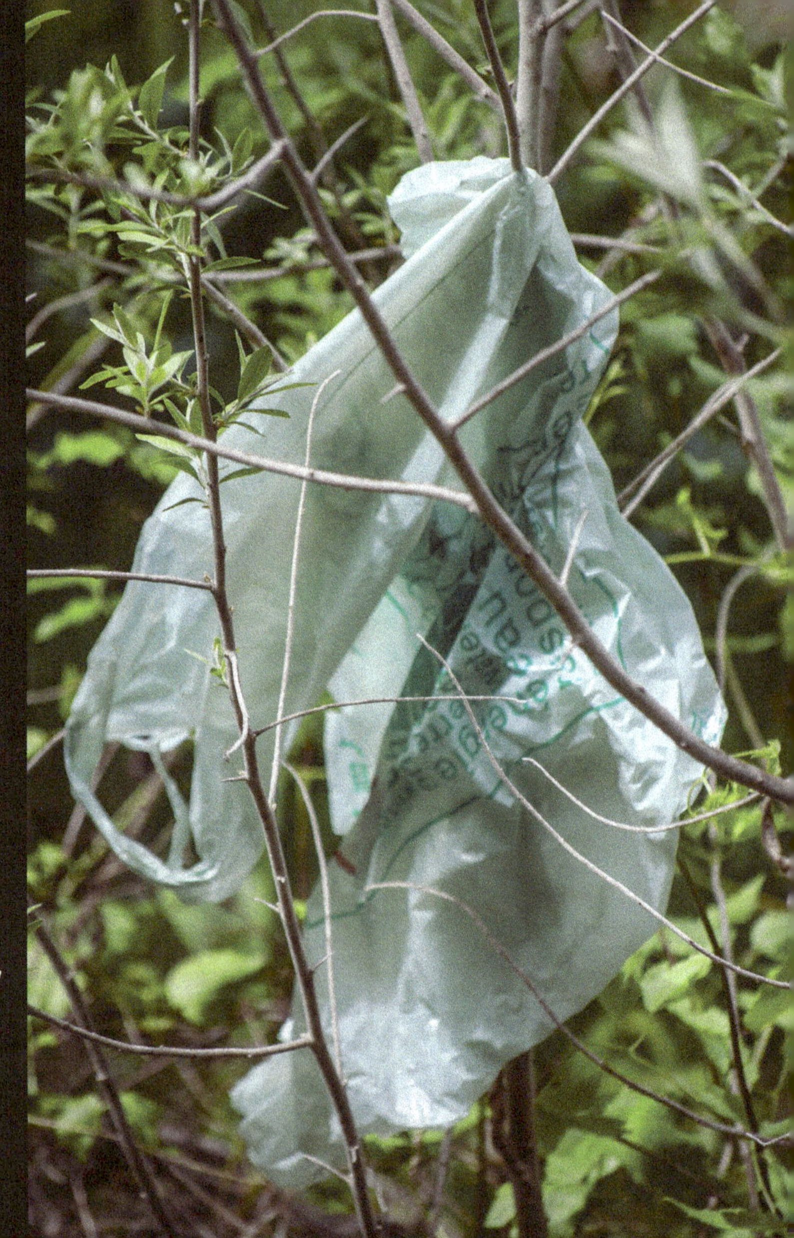

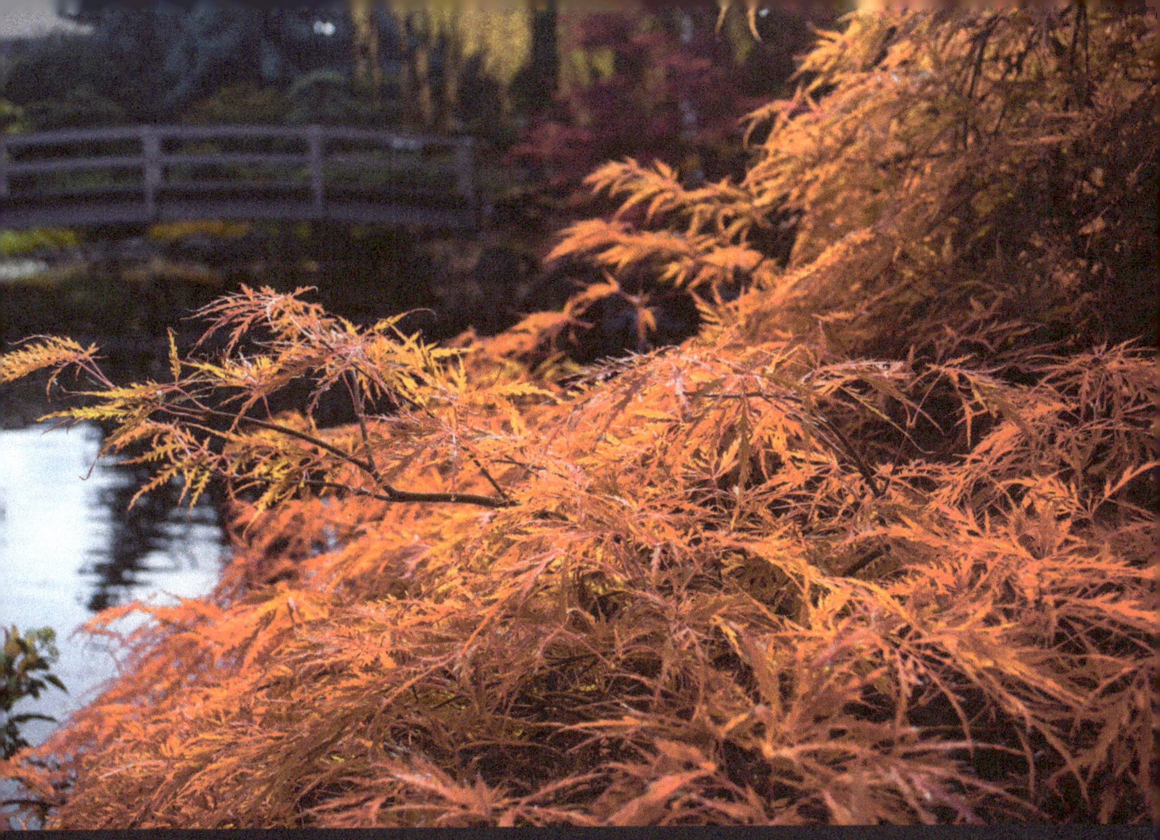

"Are you on fire?" asked Fish.

"No," laughed Tree. "I'm just wearing my brightest leaves before resting through winter."

"Hey, Shadow, thanks for the visit," sighed Sidewalk. "I miss you on cloudy days."

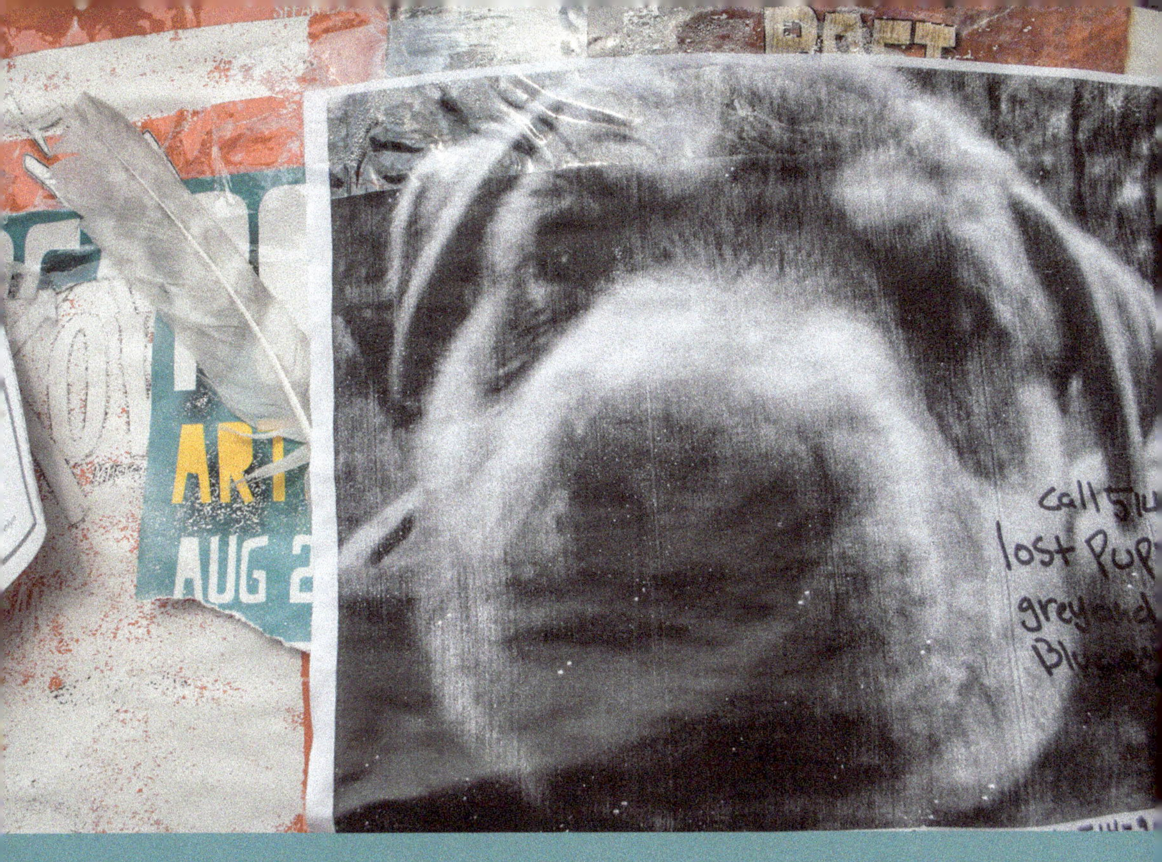

Feather screeched to a halt and tucked herself behind the poster. "Maybe if I stay here," she thought, "people will pay more attention to this lost puppy." She knew what it felt like to be separated from someone she loved. She would always miss bird.

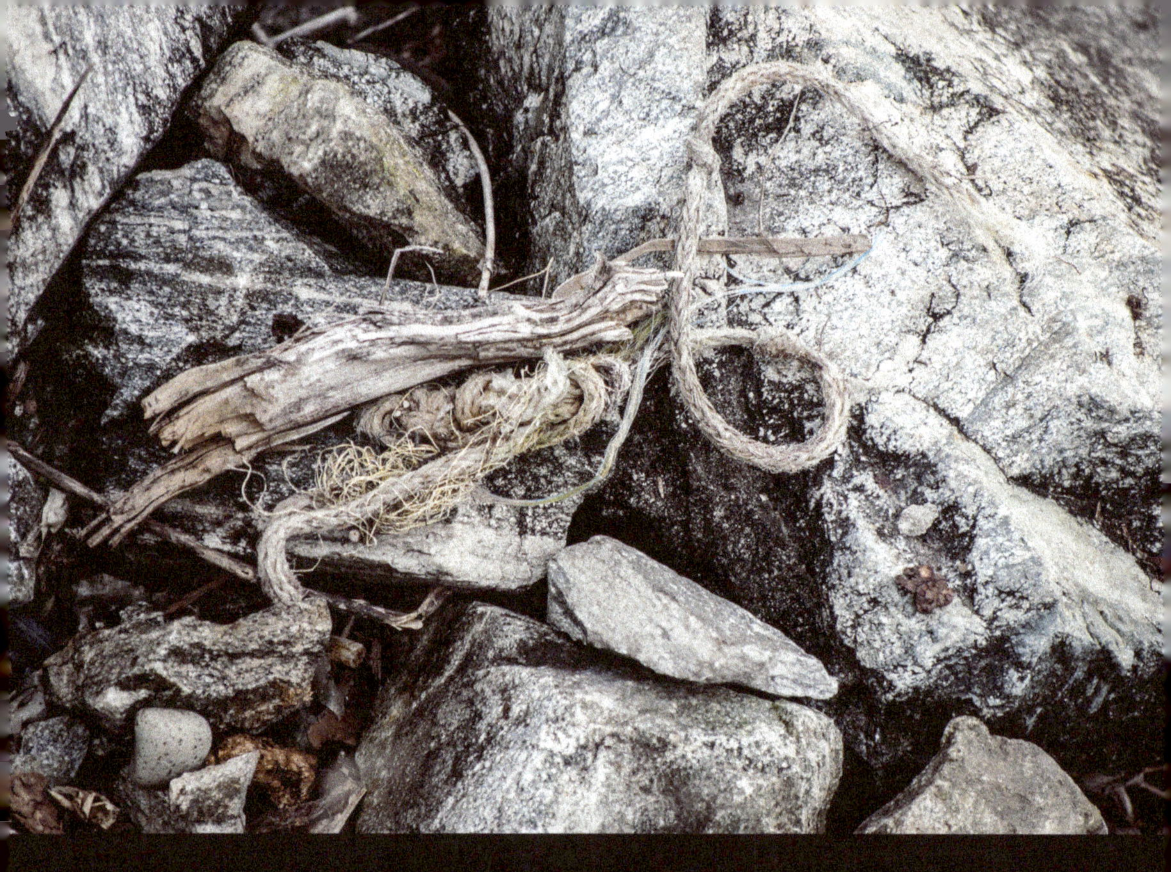

Rope and stick met after a storm deposited them atop the stones. They talked about the weather until they felt relaxed with each other. Then they dived into the deeper waters of friendship.

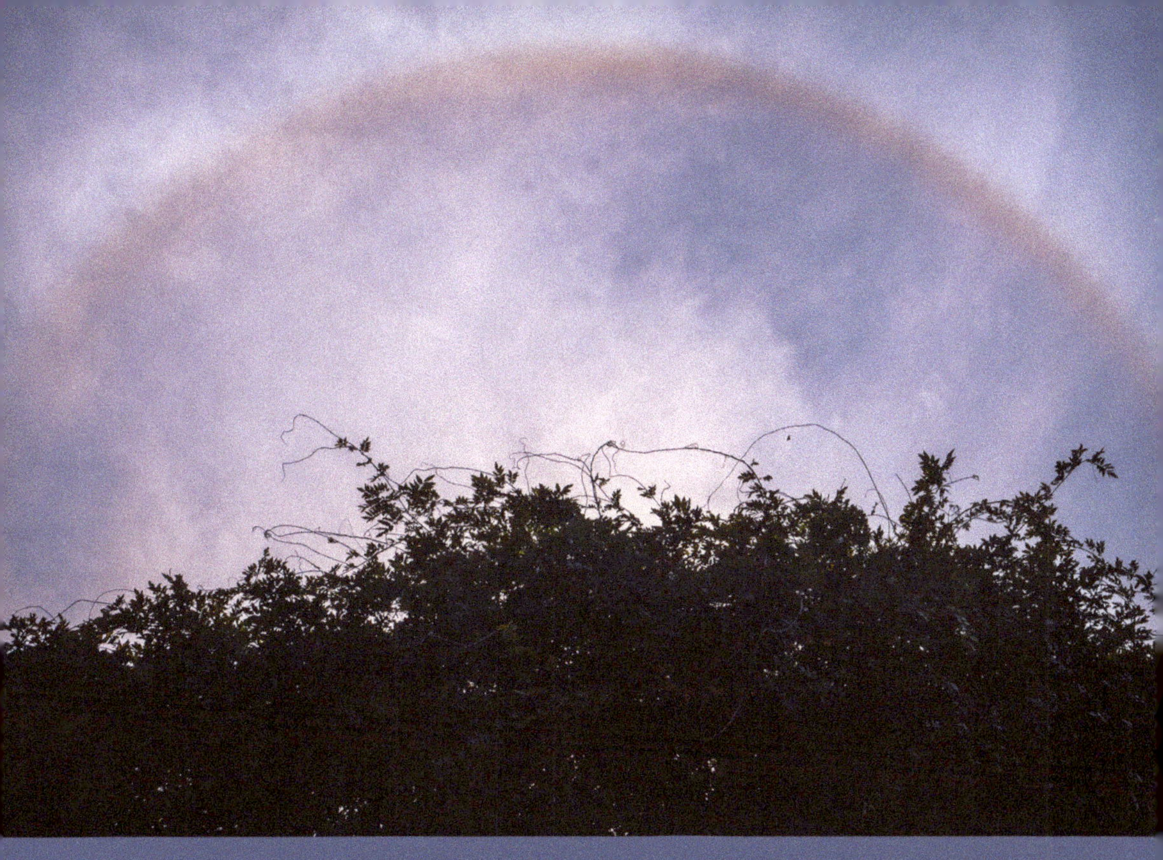

Rainbow played with clouds, making perfectly curved swaths of colour across them. Vines stretched skyward, hoping Rainbow and clouds understood how much they appreciated the show.

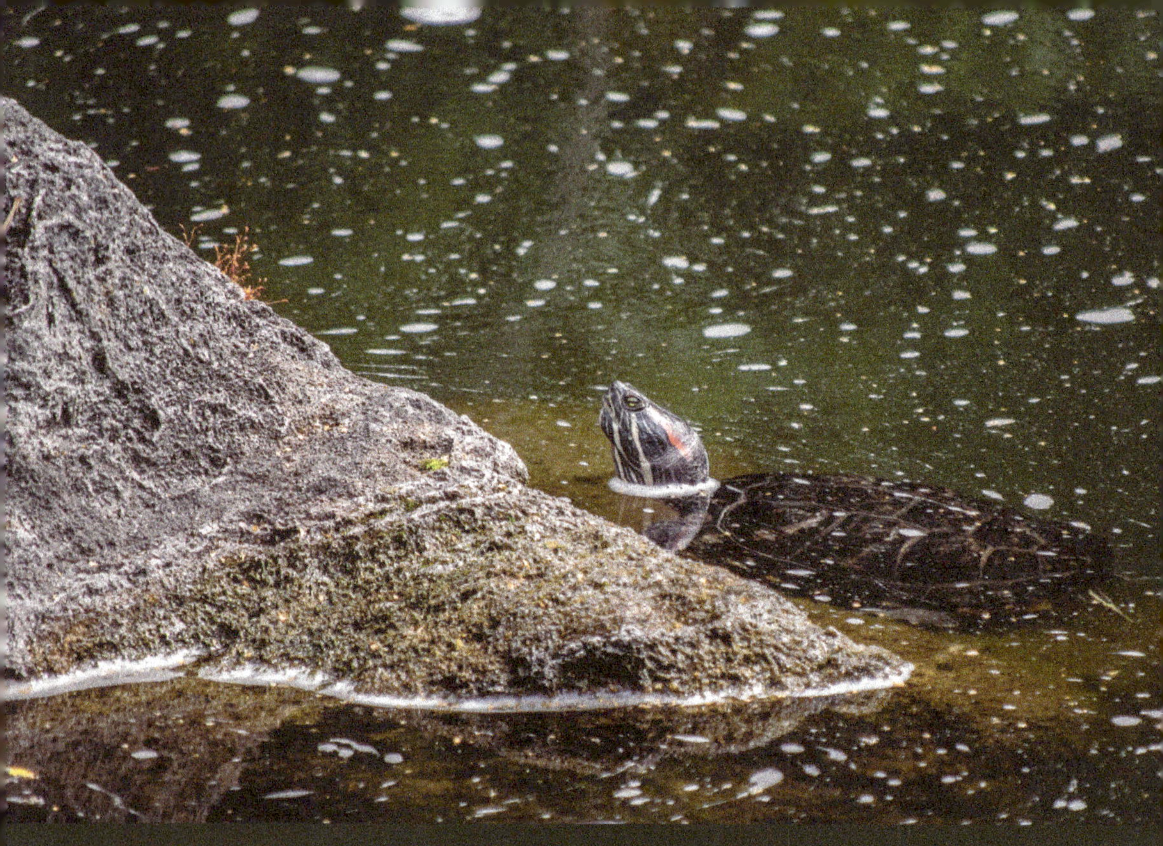

Some days the mountain was too high and too steep to climb. That's when Turtle took comfort in the familiar waters below.

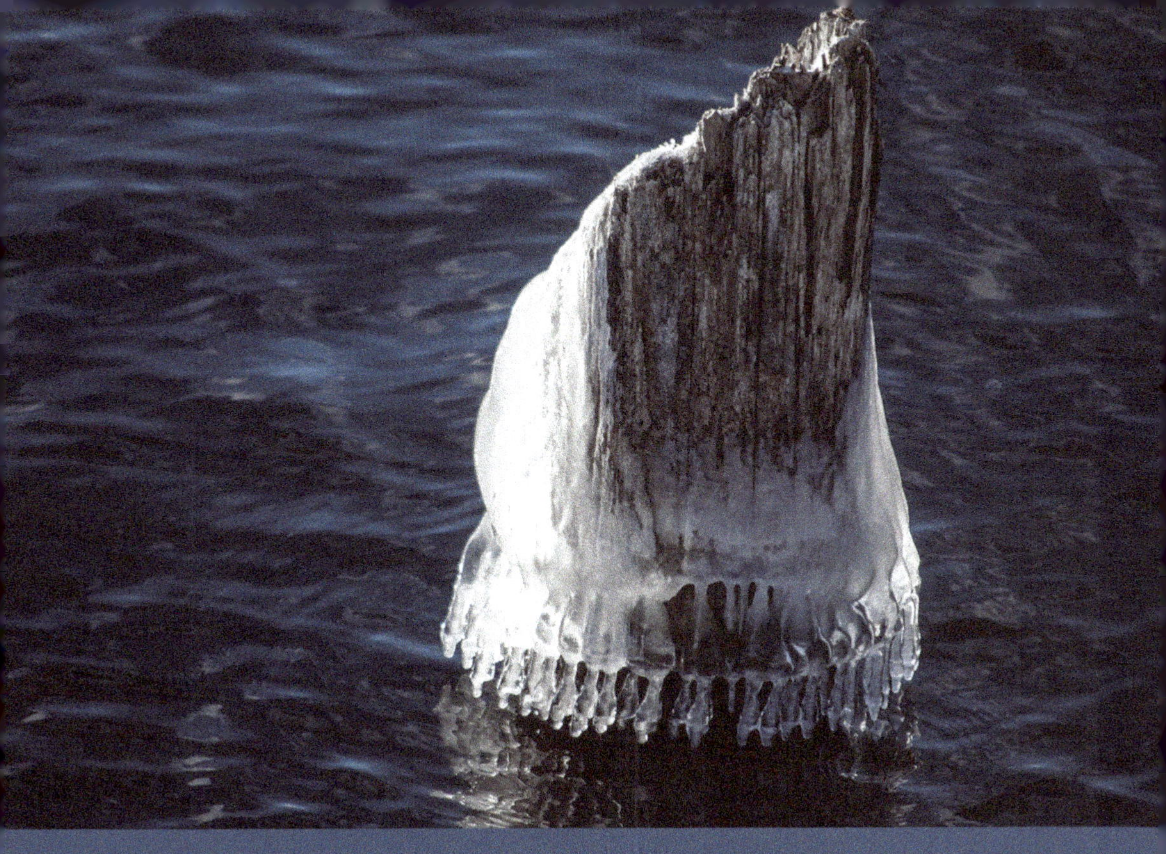

Ice gathered on the old post. Wind and waves gave him a fringe of lace. He had been a forest dweller and a dock supporter. Now he was contemplating becoming a ballet dancer.

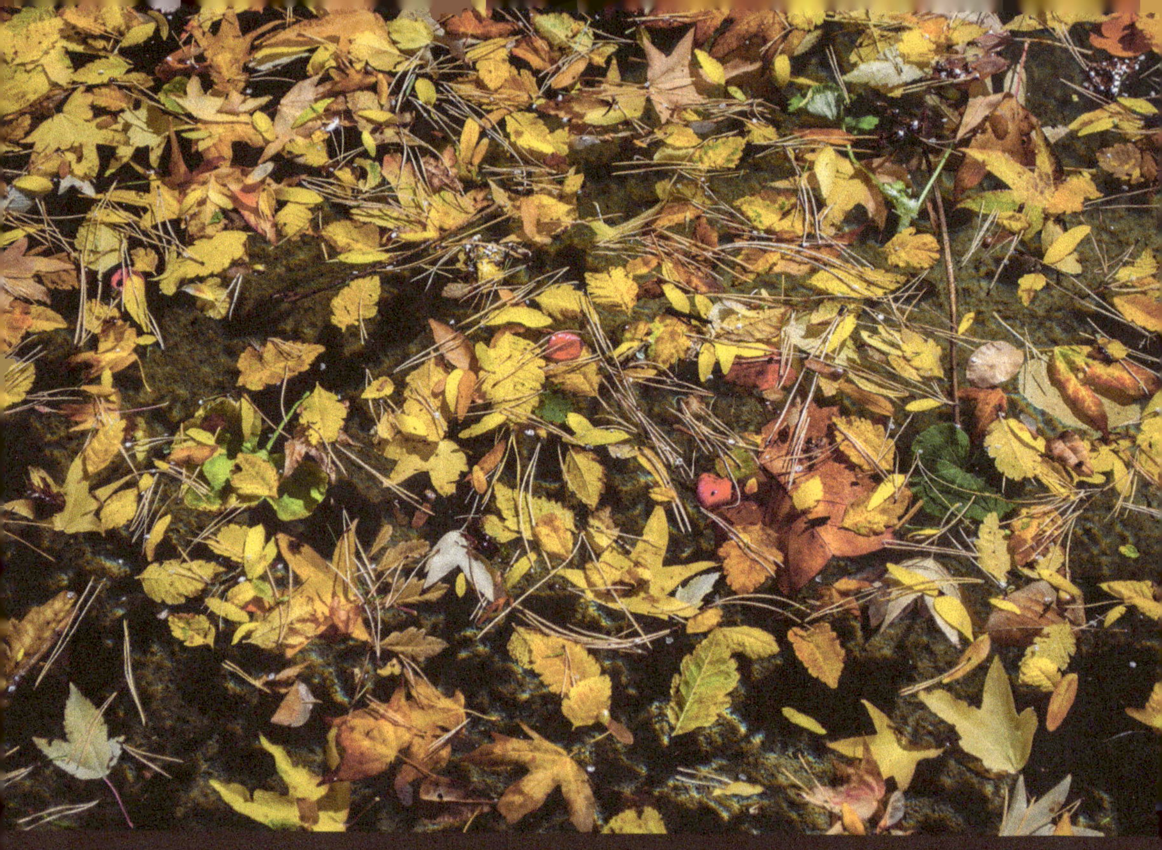

Big Orange saw she had made a mistake when she invited everyone in the neighborhood to be part of her autumn symphony. She was trying to organize the leaves by color. But they had spent all summer on different trees and were too busy visiting.

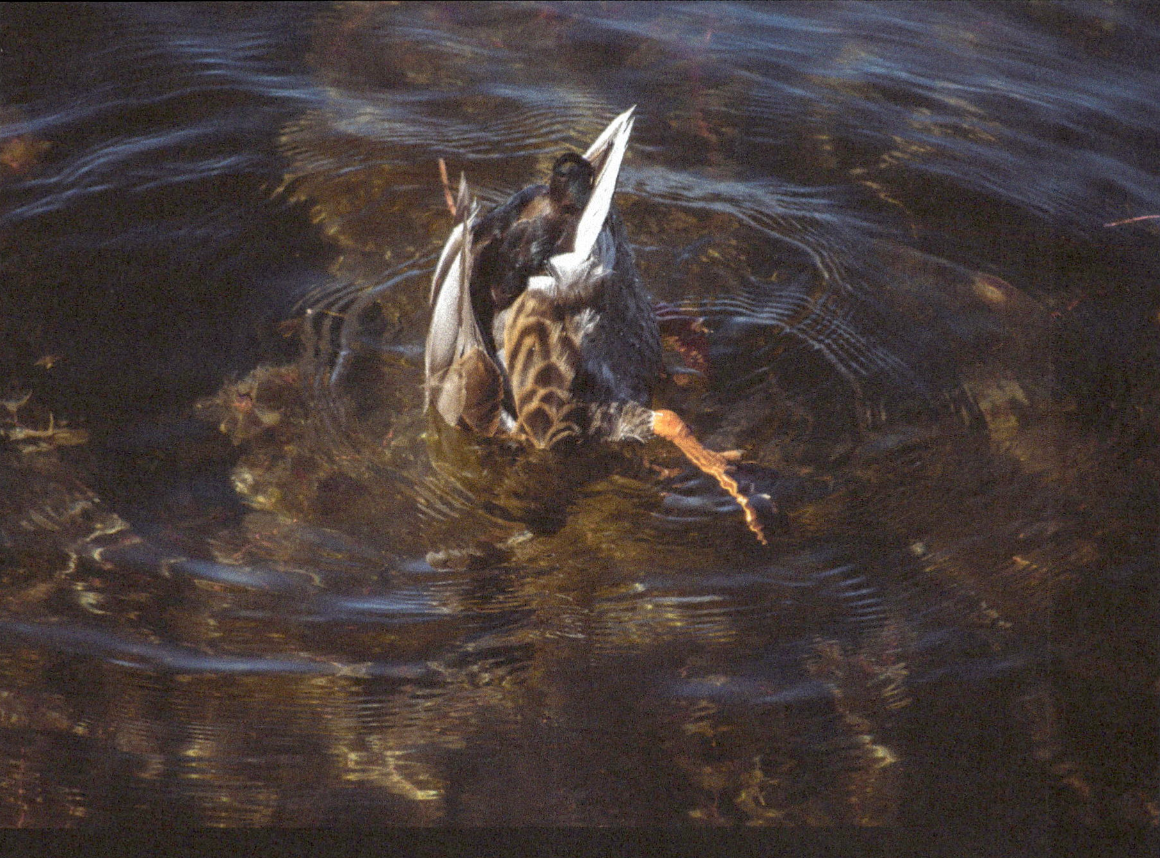

The humans saw only an invasive weed, to be pulled out and destroyed. Mallard saw yummy millefeuille and all the tasty treats hidden in her waving fronds. Perspective is everything.

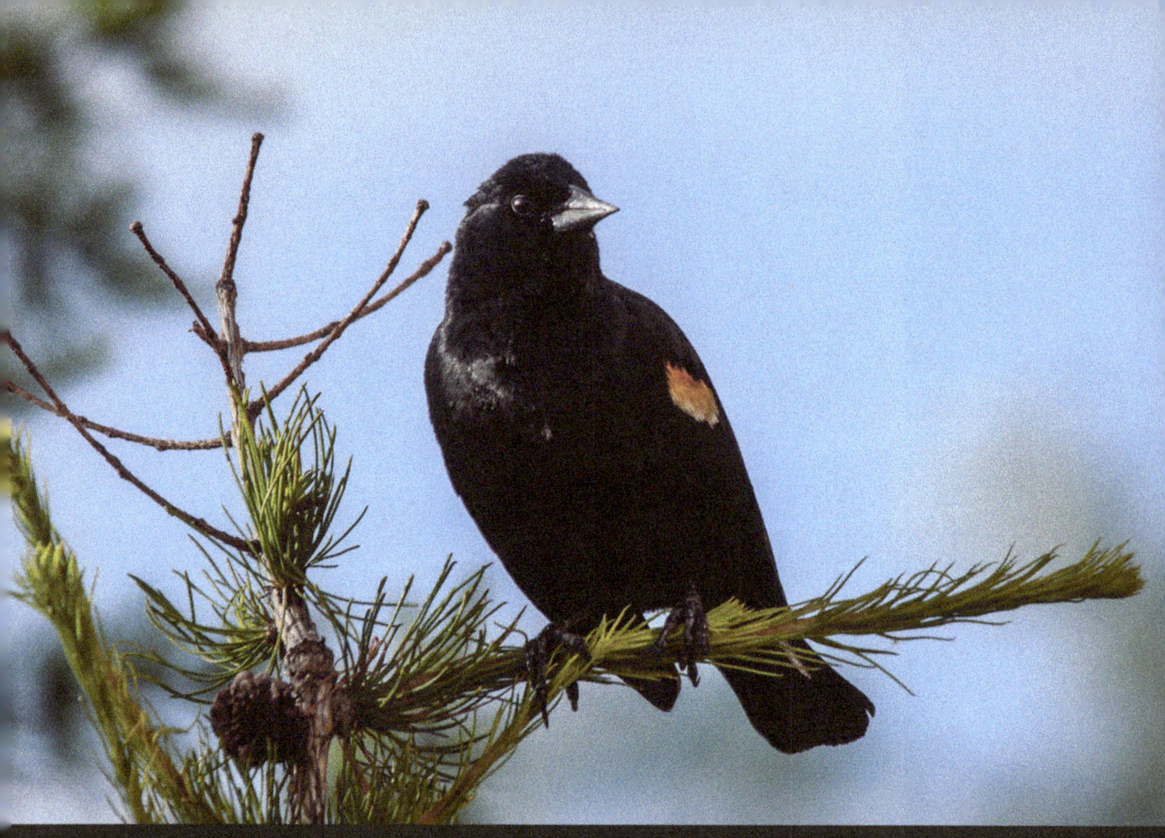

He looked serene, sitting on the tamarack. Humans never guessed he was contemplating an attack. They strolled beneath him. He sang a warning. Suddenly, they felt a whoosh and the sharp sting of claws.

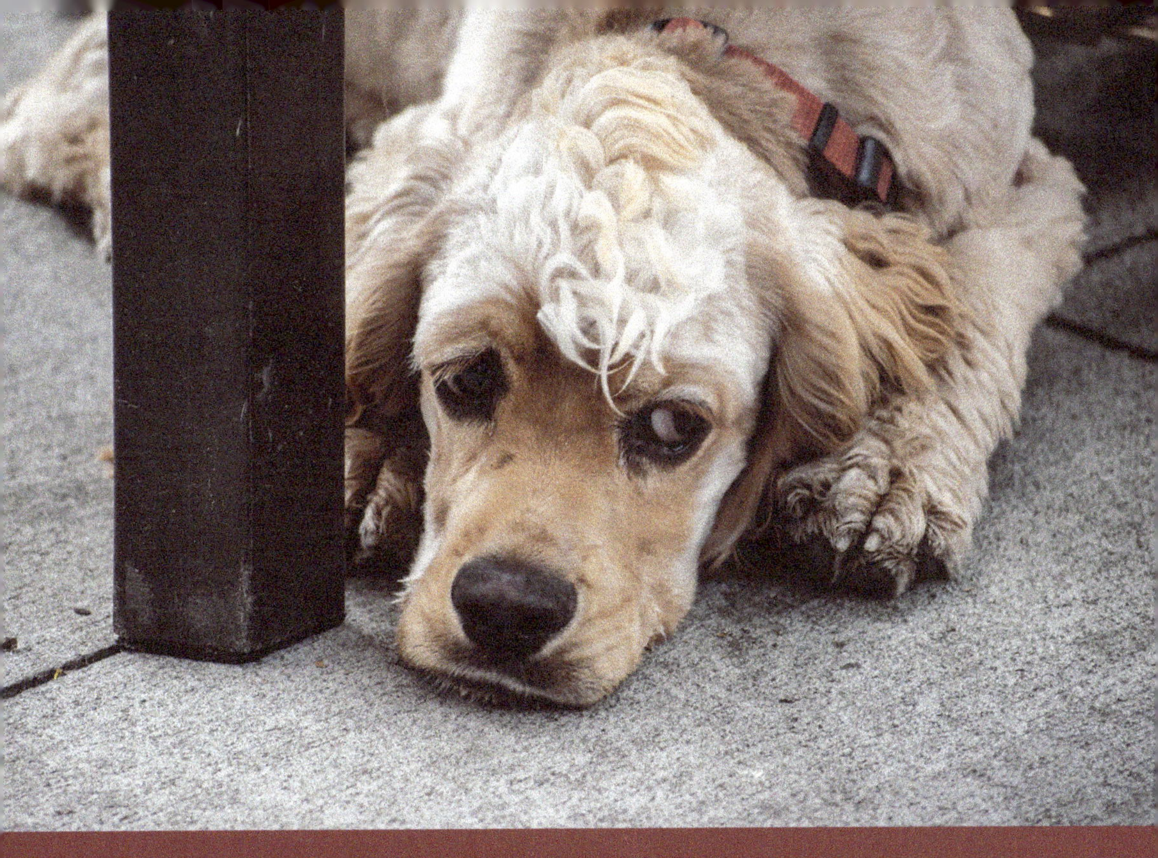

He hadn't minded the strange haircut until his human had his hair cut the same way. He was mortified to think his human was trying to look like a dog.

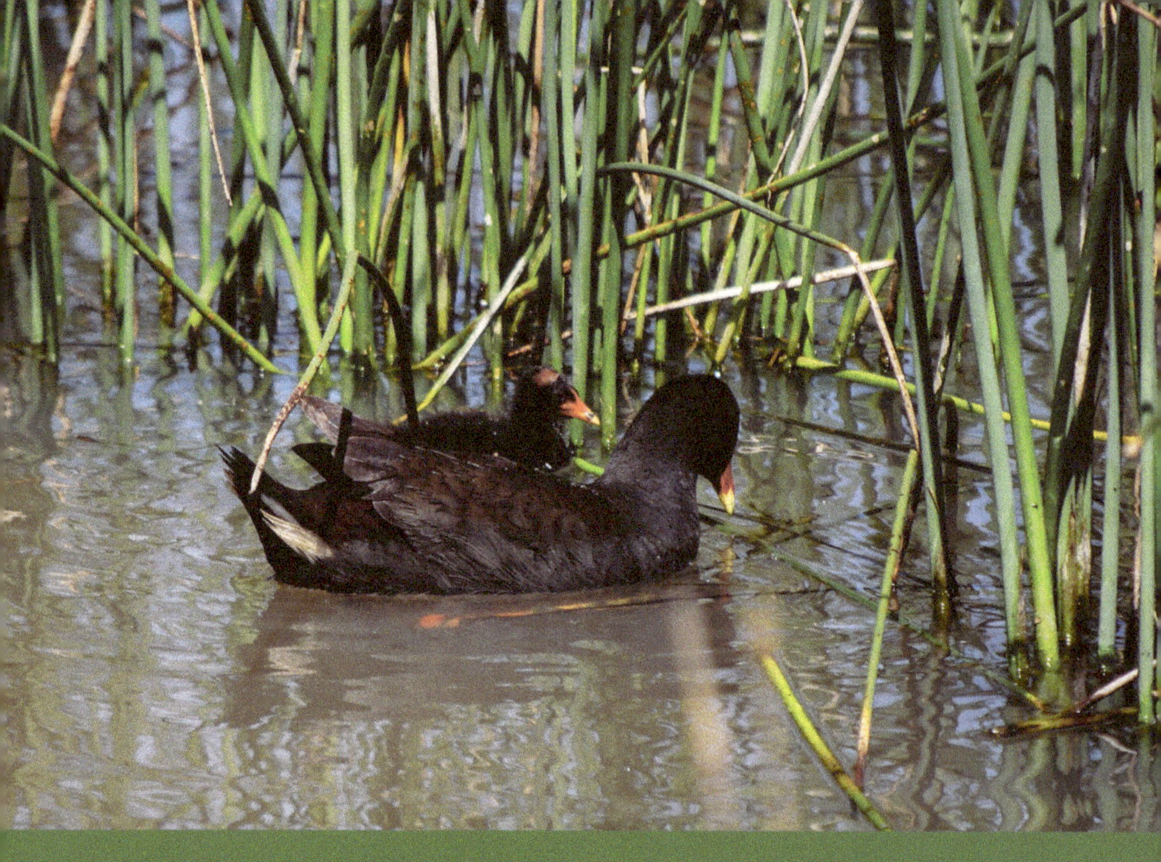

The other swamp hen chicks laughed at Mazie and called her "baldy", but her mother saw the orange patch as evidence this chick was the most special of all.

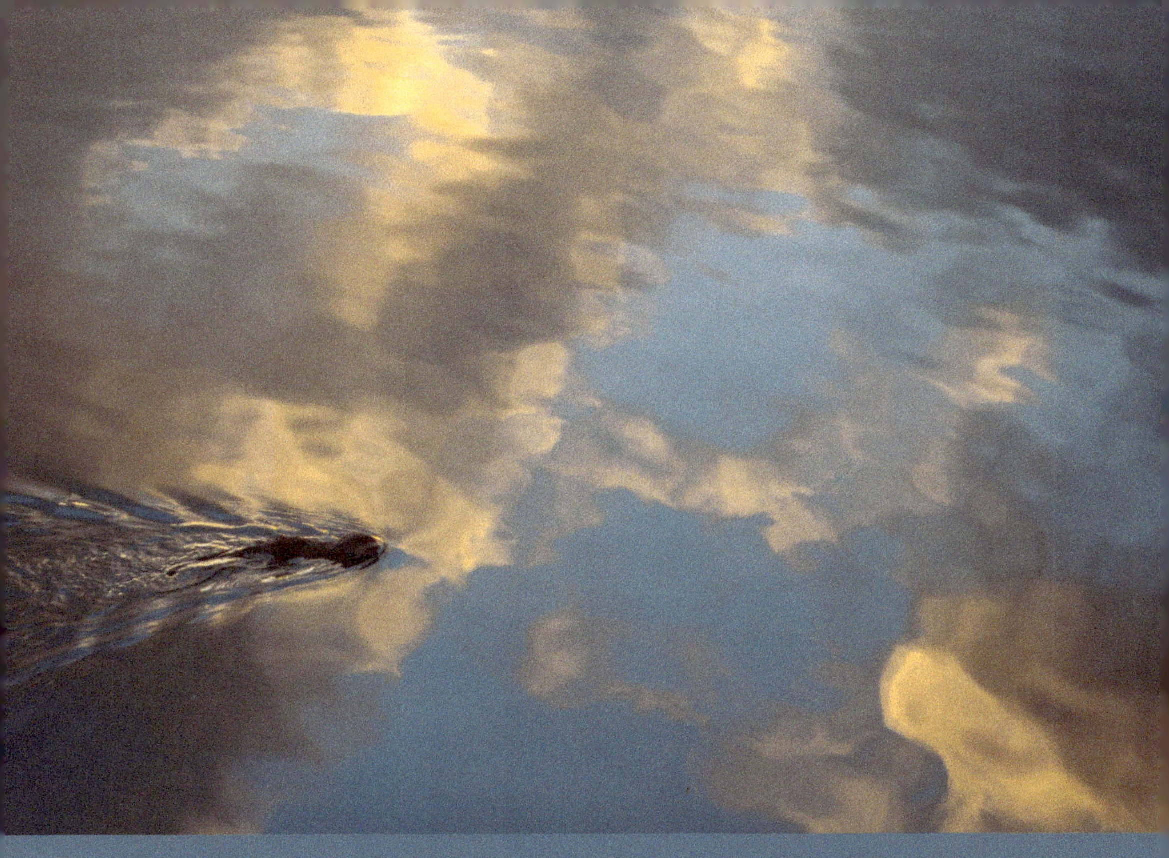

Muskrat swam toward home. To him, the lake looked and felt as it always did. To the watching humans, muskrat was an artist, cutting patterns through golden clouds.

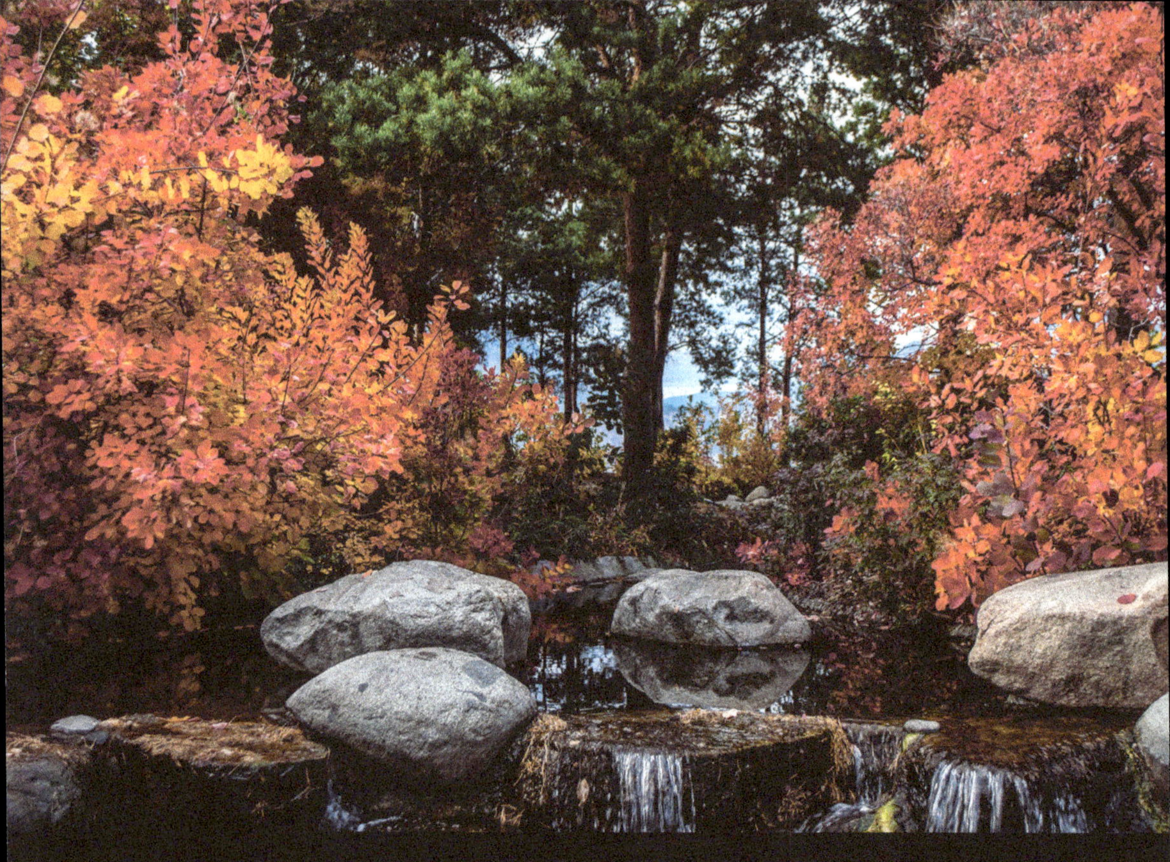

It started as a competition to see which side of the creek could shine brighter. The more they stared at each other, the happier they felt. What began as competition ended in admiration.

ABOUT THE AUTHOR

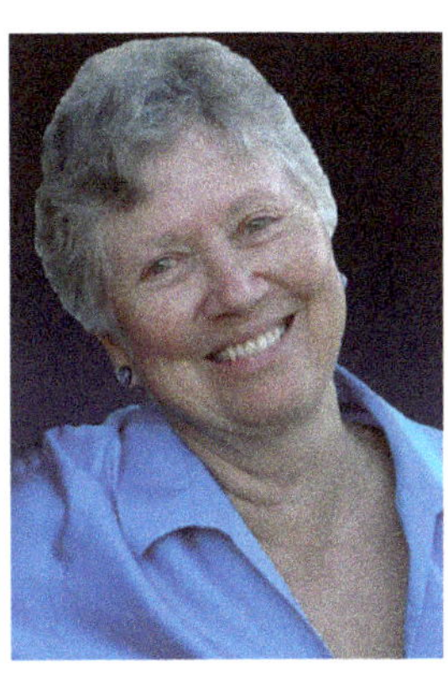

Cathryn Wellner is a writer, photographer and storyteller living in Kelowna, British Columbia, Canada. Her recent books include:

The Disappearing Pumpkin Choir
That Tree Talked to Me
Parts of Me Are Still Amazing
Hope Wins
Feisty Aging
In the Hug of Hills
Millie's Feathered Foster Family
Turkey Baby and the Hungry Hawk
Turkey Baby Finds Her Magic

You can find links to these and her other books at cathrynwellner.com. Contact her at cathryn@cathrynwellner.com or 778-478-2760. Her photographs can be found on her Web site, as well as on Facebook and Instagram.

BE A BOOK REVIEW ANGEL

If you enjoyed this book, please post a review on Amazon or Goodreads. Share it with friends and rave about it on social media. You can contact the author at cathryn@cathrynwellner.com.

Authors rely on their readers to help spread the word about books they like. People who review books are special kinds of reader angels. I guarantee when you review this book, or any other book that has given you pleasure in any way, you'll feel those wings poking out your back. Look closely in the mirror, and you might even see a halo.

Credits

Fonts used on cover and some interior pages: Saltash, BasicSans, Salt & Pepper. Font used in stories: Bw Surco. Logo font: Ed's Market. Graphic elements by Katie Pertiet and Eva Katerina. All fonts and graphic elements are licensed through DesignCuts.

Text and photographs by Cathryn Wellner. The book was designed in Photoshop.

Thank you to the creative people who designed the unique fonts and elements incorporated in this book. I continually learn from you.

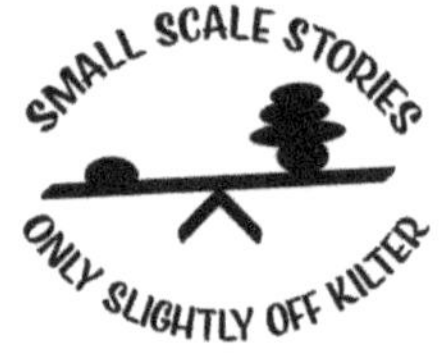